AF269847

# NOT JUST A
# BAD DAY

## Understanding Depression

**WENDY MORAGNE**
**TABITHA MORIARTY**

TWENTY-FIRST CENTURY BOOKS / MINNEAPOLIS

# CONTENT WARNING

This book contains discussions of self-harm and suicide. If you are experiencing mental health-related distress or if you are worried about a loved one who may need crisis support, you can call or text the Suicide and Crisis Lifeline at 988 or chat at 988lifeline.org. These services are confidential, free, and available twenty-four hours a day and seven days a week.

This books also contains brief mentions of and data about sexual violence. If you or a loved one have experienced or are experiencing sexual violence and are seeking help, you can call the Rape, Abuse and Incest National Network (RAINN), National Sexual Assault Hotline at 800-656-HOPE (4673), or chat online at online.rainn.org. These services are also available all day, every day.



Twenty-First Century Books™
An imprint of Lerner Publishing Group, Inc.
241 First Avenue North
Minneapolis, MN 55401 USA

For reading levels and more information, look up this title at www.lernerbooks.com.

Diagram on page 10 by Laura K. Westlund.

Main body text set in Conduit ITC Std.
Typeface provided by International Typeface Corp.

**Library of Congress Cataloging-in-Publication Data**

Names: Moragne, Wendy, author. | Moriarty, Tabitha, author.
Title: Not just a bad day : understanding depression / Wendy Moragne, Tabitha Moriarty.
Description: Minneapolis : Twenty-First Century Books , [2025] | Series: Healthy living library | Includes bibliographical references and index. | Audience: Ages 13–18 | Audience: Grades 7–9 | Summary: "More prevalent than ever, depression affects approximately 280 million people worldwide. Discover what depression is and its causes, symptoms, treatment options, and more in this timely and relevant guide"— Provided by publisher.
Identifiers: LCCN 2023047047 (print) | LCCN 2023047048 (ebook) | ISBN 9798765626986 (library binding) | ISBN 9798765630082 (paperback) | ISBN 9798765638835 (epub)
Subjects: LCSH: Depression, Mental—Juvenile literature. | Depression, Mental—Treatment—Juvenile literature.
Classification: LCC RC537 .M6695 2025 (print) | LCC RC537 (ebook) | DDC 616.85/27—dc23/eng/20240104

LC record available at https://lccn.loc.gov/2023047047
LC ebook record available at https://lccn.loc.gov/2023047048

Manufactured in the United States of America
1-1010131-52070-3/1/2024

# CONTENTS


INTRODUCTION
**WHAT IS DEPRESSION?** ———————— 4

CHAPTER ONE
**THE BASICS OF DEPRESSION** ————— 7

CHAPTER TWO
**SIGNS AND SYMPTOMS** ——————— 28

CHAPTER THREE
**DIAGNOSIS AND TREATMENT** ———— 42

CHAPTER FOUR
**SUICIDE AND ITS PREVENTION** ——— 67

CHAPTER FIVE
**FAMILY, FRIENDS, AND SCHOOL** —— 80

CHAPTER SIX
**THE POWER OF SELF-ESTEEM** ——— 89

CONCLUSION
**THE FUTURE OF DEPRESSION** ———— 98

GLOSSARY ———————————— 100
SOURCE NOTES ———————————103
SELECTED BIBLIOGRAPHY—————————104
RESOURCES ——————————— 106
FURTHER READING ————————— 108
INDEX ———————————————110

# WHAT IS DEPRESSION?

Depression is not simply feeling blue or disappointed or down in the dumps. It is not even the intense grief experienced after the death of someone close to you. Depression is much more complex. It includes a cluster of symptoms that can last a long time and affects a person's everyday functioning.

Clinical depression, also known as major depressive disorder and major depression, is depression that is serious enough to require a doctor's care. It is a mood disorder caused by a combination of genetic, biological, psychological, and environmental factors. It affects both the mind and the body, impacting someone's thoughts, feelings, behavior, and physical condition.

Major depressive disorder is often episodic in nature. This means that often when somebody is diagnosed with depression, they do not experience depression for the rest of their life without any breaks. Usually depression comes in waves, with periods of

Depression can affect anyone. But there are many treatment options available too.

relief between episodes. Some people only ever have one episode of major depression, and they never have another after they have recovered. Depressive episodes may arise on their own as part of clinical depression, or they may exist as a part of another disorder, such as bipolar disorder. Additionally, some people may suffer from persistent depressive disorder, in which they experience low-level depression for two or more years. Regardless of how a person experiences depression, treatment options such as therapy and medication are available.

This book will discuss depression from many different angles. It will discuss the signs and symptoms of depression as well as who develops depression and why. It will also cover treatments for depression, including medication and therapy, and things that may be preventive against developing depression, such as supportive networks of family and friends or high self-esteem.

# CHAPTER ONE

# THE BASICS OF DEPRESSION

## Who Has Depression?

Depression can occur in anyone regardless of their gender, race, age, or socioeconomic class. It occurs around the world and affects millions of people, some more severely than others. Depression often runs in families, so people who are depressed are more likely to have a biological parent, sibling, grandparent, aunt, uncle, or cousin who also suffers from depression. The disorder can often be traced through several generations of a family.

The World Health Organization is a United Nations agency that helps governments around the world improve their health services. According to the organization, depression affects about 280 million people, or about 3.8 percent of the population worldwide, at any given time. The US experiences higher rates of depression than the global rate. In 2019 the Centers for Disease Control and Prevention (CDC) reported that at least 18.5 percent of US adults reported experiencing any signs or symptoms of depression, with about 7.0 percent of adults experiencing moderate or severe symptoms of depression. Then in 2020, about 8.4 percent of US adults experienced at least one major depressive episode. This number was higher in part due to the COVID-19 pandemic, which began to affect the United States in early 2020. More people experienced depression during the pandemic for a variety of reasons, including social isolation, increased stress over world events, deaths of loved ones, and fear of getting sick, among others.

Rates of depression can vary among different genders, races, ethnicities, and socioeconomic statuses. The National Center for Health Statistics from the CDC published a report in 2018 analyzing the differences between depression rates in various groups of people from 2013 to 2016. They found that:

- Women (10.4 percent) were almost twice as likely as men (5.5 percent) to have had depression.
- There was no statistically significant difference in rates of depression among different age groups.
- The prevalence of depression was lowest among non-Hispanic Asian adults (3.1 percent).
- Non-Hispanic Black adults had the highest rates of depression (9.2 percent), followed by Hispanic adults (8.2 percent) and non-Hispanic white adults (7.9 percent), although the differences in these rates were not statistically significant.
- The prevalence of depression among adults decreased as family or household income levels increased.

- Eighty percent of people with depression reported that their symptoms made it difficult to perform at work or school, complete chores and other tasks, or get along with other people.

It is important to note that this study did not include people who were currently in nursing homes or other institutions, which have higher rates of depression and other mental illnesses than the general population. It also does not account for people who may be less likely to report symptoms of depression due to cultural differences in how mental illnesses are perceived and talked about.

Additionally, this study did not look specifically at levels of depression in LGBTQ+ youth. The Trevor Project, an organization that focuses on suicide prevention in LGBTQ+ youth, reported that in 2022, 58 percent of LGBTQ+ youth reported experiencing symptoms of depression. The rates were highest among transgender youth (people whose gender identity differs from the gender they were assigned at birth) and nonbinary youth (people whose gender identity is neither solely woman nor man) at nearly 66 percent.

## ADOLESCENTS AND DEPRESSION

The 2021 National Survey on Drug Use and Health stated that 1 in 5 adolescents between the ages of twelve and seventeen had experienced a major depressive episode that year. Out of these teens, at least 75 percent had symptoms that were so severe that they were unable to function how they usually would at home, at school, or in their friendships. More than half of these teenagers did not receive treatment for their depression.

What may appear to be normal struggles through the teenage years may in fact be depression. In 2019 a national survey of

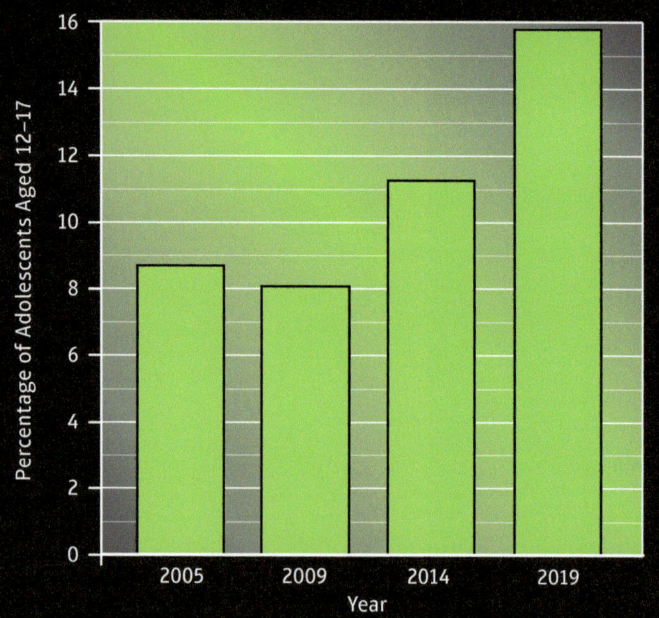


The prevalence of depression in people between the ages of twelve and seventeen is steadily increasing. It almost doubled between 2005 and 2019, and, as of 2023, has continued to rise.

adolescents between the age of twelve and seventeen found that 15.8 percent of them were depressed. This is a big increase in the number of teens with depression from 2009, when the rate of depression among teens was estimated to be about 8.1 percent. Experts from the Child Mind Institute, a non-profit organization dedicated to helping young people struggling with mental health, believe that social media use has contributed to the increase of depression and other mental illnesses in young people in the US. This may be from time spent online taking away from time spent connecting with others in person or working on other hobbies that help them feel good, such as exercising, playing instruments, or making art. Research shows that teenagers who spend more time on social media feel more isolated and have worse self-esteem.

But many experts believe social media isn't the only reason rates of depression have increased. Other increased pressures on teens in the 2020s include growing pressures to perform academically and chronic stress from the COVID-19 pandemic. They

Young people face many social and political stressors and often help lead movements for change. The modern pressures they face may be contributing to increasing rates of depression and other mental illnesses among their age group.

# TEEN GIRLS AND LGBTQ+ TEENS IN THE US

A 2023 CDC report highlighted US teen girls and members of the LGBTQ+ community as being at particularly high risk for sexual violence and deteriorating mental health. The data shows that 57 percent of US teen girls reported feeling persistently sad or hopeless in 2021, which was a 60 percent increase over the decade prior.

In addition to the increase in depression, US teen girls are facing more violence and thoughts of self-harm than in previous years. The report found that:

- Nearly 1 in 3 (30%) seriously considered attempting suicide in 2021.
- 1 in 5 experienced sexual violence within the past year.
- 14 percent had been forced to have nonconsensual sex, or rape, within the past year.

also face increased stress from tense political climates, increased awareness of climate change, and uncertainty about the future.

## Rates of Recovery

Once somebody has experienced their first episode of depression, there is about a 50 percent chance that they will have another depressive episode at some point in their lifetime. The other 50 percent of people will not experience another depressive episode. For

Members of the LGBTQ+ community are also facing more violence and depression, likely due in part to governmental policy changes and increased public attacks against the LGBTQ+ communities and identities. Focusing specifically on LGBQ+ students, the CDC report states that in 2021:

- More than half (52%) had recently experienced poor mental health.
- More than two-thirds (69%) experienced persistent sadness or hopelessness.
- More than 1 in 5 (22%) attempted suicide within the past year.
- More than 1 in 5 (22%) experienced sexual violence.

These increases in sexual violence and mental health struggles are serious challenges facing teens. Many factors such as the COVID-19 pandemic, changing social and political climates, and the continuing influence of social media have played a part in the current youth mental health crisis.

those who do have recurring episodes of depression, new episodes often tend to be longer and more severe than the previous ones.

When people receive proper treatment, about 30 percent of them achieve full recovery or remission—the reduction or disappearance of the signs and symptoms of a disorder, illness, or disease. About 20 percent of people with major depression will have some improvement in their symptoms, but will not get rid of them completely, and about 50 percent of people with depression will not respond to treatment at all. For teenagers with depression

who seek treatment, about 60 percent of them see at least a
50 percent decrease in their symptoms within twelve weeks of
treatment. The 40 percent who do not get better in the first twelve
weeks are determined to have treatment-resistant depression,
which is depression that does not respond much or at all to common
treatments such as therapy or antidepressant medications. Their
depression may even get worse during treatment. Treatment-
resistant depression has been associated with many possible
causes, such as increased time on the internet and social media, but
researchers don't know the exact cause of it. We'll talk more about
treatments for depression, including those for treatment-resistant
depression, in chapter three.

## What Are the Signs and Symptoms of Depression?

People who are depressed may feel sad or irritable or may lose
interest in activities or hobbies that once gave them pleasure.
Many feel overly tired or anxious, and most feel worthless and
hopeless. Depression can interfere with sleeping and eating and can
cause headaches and stomachaches. It can cause argumentative
behavior, aggression, or the desire to be alone, all of which can
strain relationships with family, household members, and friends.
Depression can also interfere with concentration and memory, which
can cause a drop in school or job performance. Some depressed
individuals even have thoughts of death and suicide.

Although many people experience some symptoms of
depression from time to time, that does not necessarily mean they
have major depressive disorder. It is normal to have ups and downs
in your mood, concentration, and the way you interact with other

An increase in anger, aggression, or argumentative behavior can be a sign of depression, especially when coupled with other symptoms.

people. If someone experiences a lot of depression symptoms at once, and the symptoms last for two weeks or more, then that is when they can be diagnosed with clinical depression. If their symptoms have not lasted two weeks yet, they may still have depression, but they will not have met the threshold for diagnosis.

Symptoms of depression vary from one person to another. The combination of symptoms present in one person may not be the same combination present in another person. The severity of the symptoms and the length of time they are present also vary.

When a person suffers from depression, the symptoms they experience and the pain they feel can lead to disruptive behavior, challenges at school, social problems, and alcohol and drug use. Giving up a favorite sport or other activity, cutting school, or fighting with siblings may be signs of depression. Even repeatedly declining invitations to get together with friends may signal depression.

# Depression in the Brain

People used to think that depression only occurred from a chemical imbalance in the brain. But this is not quite true. In fact, researchers still aren't exactly sure why depression occurs. A chemical imbalance can be involved, but there are many other possible causes of depression, such as genetic vulnerability, stressful life events, and an inability of the brain to regulate a person's mood. Different cases of depression may have different combinations of causes too.

Some of the symptoms of depression can result from an abnormality in the way the brain produces and maintains the levels of certain chemicals that help transmit messages between nerve cells. The brain is composed of billions of nerve cells called neurons. Each of these has hundreds or thousands of interconnections with other neurons. Neurons in the brain communicate with one another by sending electrical signals, or messages, through axons—long, thin, stemlike projections found on neurons.

At the end of axons are branchlike nerve endings called dendrites that contain storage sacs called vesicles. These storage sacs release chemicals called neurotransmitters. Neurotransmitters carry the message across the tiny fluid-filled gap, or synapse, that separates the nerve endings on the axon from the body of the next neuron. When the message crosses the synapse and reaches receptors on the next neuron, the receptors are activated, which in turn activate the neuron.

In the past, research on depression has been fairly slow because the brain is complex, and it is difficult to study brain tissue in a living person without harming them. However, increasingly sophisticated technology has allowed researchers to look at brain

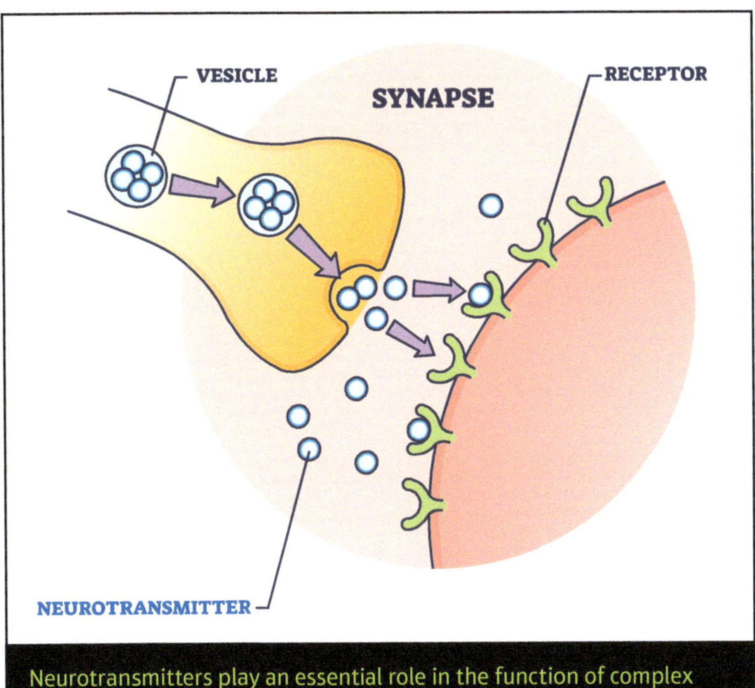



Neurotransmitters play an essential role in the function of complex neural systems by moving messages between neurons.

activity without harming the people involved. Positron emission tomography and single-photon emission computed tomography are imaging techniques through which researchers can map the brain and see which areas have the highest density of neurotransmitter receptors, usually meaning that these areas have the most activity. Functional magnetic resonance imaging is a special type of scan that allows researchers to watch the brain in action as it performs different tasks and identify the different parts of the brain involved.

The parts of the brain that play a significant role in depression are the amygdala, which often regulates fear and anger; the thalamus, which regulates many functions of the body such as temperature, heart rate, hunger, and activity levels; and the hippocampus, which plays an important role in learning and memory. Some depressed people even have a smaller hippocampus than people of similar ages who are not depressed.

# What Causes Depression?

Ongoing research indicates that depression is likely caused by a combination of genetic, biological, psychological, and environmental factors.

## GENETIC FACTORS

Since depression tends to run in families in the same way that heart disease or diabetes does, researchers believe that some people have a genetic vulnerability to developing this disorder. Young people who have a depressed biological parent, grandparent, or sibling are at the greatest risk for developing depression. However, it is important to note that being at risk for developing depression does not mean that an individual is sure to develop it. Likewise, sometimes depression occurs in people who have no family history of the disorder.

Heredity, or the genetics someone inherits from their biological parents and grandparents, plays a part in a person's psychological makeup. Some people are naturally upbeat and optimistic, while others are more prone to overthinking and lower mood. Those who think pessimistically, worry excessively, and have a poor self-image may be prone to developing depression. Those who are introverted or extremely dependent on others also tend to be at greater risk of developing depression.

Scientists are studying the brain and depression to find out exactly what aspect of depression is inherited. Some researchers are searching for a specific gene that, if identified, would explain why certain people develop depression while others do not. Other researchers have been studying whether certain abnormalities in the brain's chemical makeup can be passed on from generation to generation. Current research suggests that about 50 percent of the cause of most cases of depression is genetic, and about 50 percent is due to either psychological or physical factors.

## BIOLOGICAL FACTORS

Neurotransmitters, the brain chemicals that carry messages from one neuron to another, affect behavior, thoughts, and feelings. Dopamine, norepinephrine, and serotonin are all neurotransmitters. There appears to be a relationship between these chemicals and specific symptoms of major depressive disorder. When the levels of these brain chemicals are out of balance, the brain cannot function properly. Norepinephrine and serotonin regulate mood. More specifically, norepinephrine regulates alertness, so when there is an inadequate amount in the brain, symptoms such as fatigue and a sad mood result. Serotonin regulates sleep, appetite, motor activity, and aggression. When there is an inadequate amount of serotonin in the brain, symptoms such as sleeplessness, irritability, and anxiety result. These are common symptoms of depression.

Although low serotonin levels have been linked to the symptoms of depression, researchers no longer believe that low serotonin is what causes depression. The role that serotonin plays in depression and the symptoms that come from an imbalance of it are still under debate, and research is ongoing. Dr. Joanna Moncrieff, a psychiatrist and professor at University College London, explains, "The serotonin theory is very old and has been very popular since the '90s, when the pharmaceutical industry started promoting it. . . . But since about

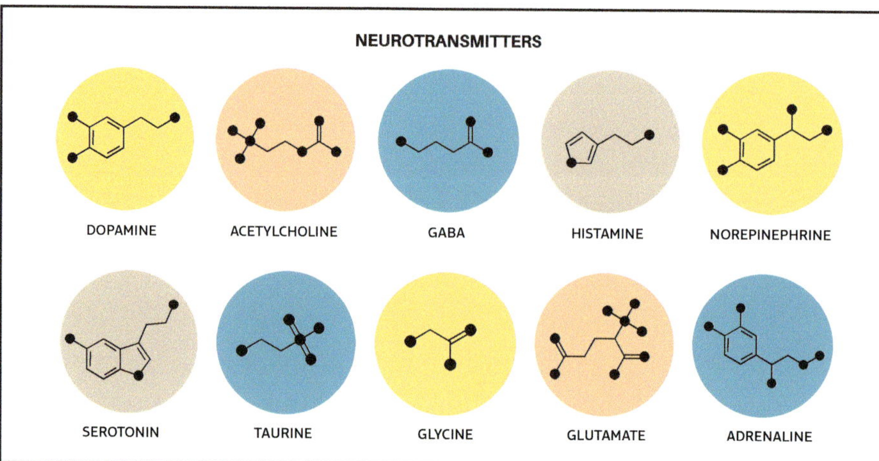



Different neurotransmitters have different functions and structures. There are over one hundred types of them in the human body, but some of the most common include adrenaline, which may increase when people are stressed or afraid, and dopamine, serotonin, and norepinephrine, which are all thought to be associated with certain disorders, including depression.

2005 . . . there's been sort of rumours that actually the evidence isn't very strong, or it's inconsistent. Some studies are positive, some studies are negative, but no one's really got that evidence together anywhere. . . . Evidence from placebo-controlled trials show that antidepressants are a little bit better than a sugar tablet. And if that little difference is not to do with rectifying a chemical imbalance, improving low serotonin levels, what is it to do with?"

Research has indicated that there is a hereditary component to brain chemistry, which could be another explanation of why depression tends to run in families. We know that brain chemicals can regulate mood and the creation of new connections between neurons. If brain chemistry can be inherited, then this could help explain why depression tends to occur frequently in some biological families and infrequently in others. Psychological and environmental factors, including negative thinking, stress, and traumatic life events, can also alter the brain chemistry and neural connections in certain people.

## PSYCHOLOGICAL FACTORS

Teenagers often want to fit in and to belong to a group. Having either an argumentative and explosive or a shy and insecure personality can make it feel difficult to form friendships and can limit participation in social events. The feelings of loneliness and isolation that often result can lead to poor self-esteem and depression. Young people who lack support and praise from the adults in their lives, those whose peers reject them, and those who struggle with schoolwork often feel a sense of defeat and failure. Many feel frustrated and angry. Some become critical of themselves and see the world as a gloomy place with a dark future. Negative thinking and pessimism often also lead to guilt and despair. Sometimes these young people end up feeling helpless and hopeless. They feel that things are beyond their control. This sequence of events and emotions is an example of how some social and environmental factors can play into the development and experience of depression in teenagers and adults.

## ENVIRONMENTAL FACTORS

Life events can trigger depression. The death of a loved one; chronic illness of a family member; a breakup or divorce; physical, sexual, or emotional abuse; poverty; or discrimination can bring on depression in those who are already genetically vulnerable. These hardships can even cause depression in people who do not have a family history of the disorder. Moving to a new town, pressure to get good grades, a falling-out with a friend, a break up with a romantic partner, ridicule by classmates, and other challenging events can also trigger depression.

Additionally, many teenagers face peer pressure, romantic and sexual issues, increased responsibilities at home, and friction with their parents or caregivers, all of which can be stressful and may lead to depression. Occasionally, depression develops without a trigger, meaning that some people become depressed without having faced trauma or stress.

# Types of Depression

There are several types of clinical depression. Persistent sadness and a loss of interest in things that an individual once enjoyed characterize all of them. All forms affect the individual's daily functioning. The three main types of depression are major depression; dysthymia, or chronic depression; and bipolar disorder, formerly called manic depression.

## MAJOR DEPRESSION

In major depression, symptoms are intense and last two or more weeks. They occur daily, sometimes lasting for most of the day, and impair functioning. This may look like a person being unable to get out of bed, perform their job, feed themselves, or shower. For a person to be diagnosed with major depression, symptoms cannot result from recreational or prescribed drugs or a medical condition. Sixty percent of people who have one episode of major depression will have another episode of major depression at some point in their life.

## DYSTHYMIA

Dysthymia is a milder form of depression that lasts two or more years. Dysthymia occurs gradually, and people may not be able to pinpoint when they started feeling depressed. They may also have times when they are not depressed. These so-called "normal" periods can last up to two months. Symptoms of dysthymia include eating or sleeping too much or too little, fatigue, poor concentration, difficulty making decisions, low self-esteem, and hopelessness. Young people with dysthymia often appear gloomy, irritable, and angry, and they tend to talk about feeling unloved and worthless. Some people who suffer from dysthymia later develop major depression or bipolar disorder. One study that followed people with dysthymia over 10 years showed that approximately 75 percent of people with this disorder will eventually experience remission.

## BIPOLAR DEPRESSION

People with bipolar disorder experience episodes of mania (elevated mood and energy) or hypomania (mania that is less severe) scattered throughout periods of their normal mood and functioning. They may also experience episodes of depression. Symptoms of major depression such as sadness, irritability, loss of energy, and changes in appetite characterize the low mood. Extreme happiness, great energy, a decreased need for sleep, rapid talking, grandiose ideas and plans, and inappropriate and often risky behavior characterize the elevated mood. Depressive and manic episodes, both of which are extreme, can last for days, weeks, or months. The less extreme hypomanic episodes last for less time.

There are two types of true bipolar disorder and an additional related disorder. Bipolar disorder may be split into bipolar I and bipolar II. Bipolar I is diagnosed when somebody has experienced a manic episode. Bipolar II is characterized by episodes of both hypomania and severe depression. Somebody could have bipolar I without ever having had a depressive episode, as long as they have had at least one manic episode. On the other hand, somebody could experience multiple hypomanic and depressive episodes for most of their life and be diagnosed with bipolar II. But if they ever had a manic episode, even later in life, their diagnosis would become bipolar I.

Cyclothymia is a related disorder that is characterized by multiple periods of elevated mood interspersed with depressed mood lasting at least two years. But with cyclothymia, the episodes of elevated mood do not fulfill criteria for mania, and the periods of low mood do not meet criteria for depression.

## Other Types of Depression

Some types of depression either express unique symptoms or result from specific experiences or time periods. These include:

### ATYPICAL DEPRESSION

Atypical means "not typical." Also called depression with atypical features, atypical depression is a specifier that a professional may apply to an existing depression diagnosis. The specifier helps describe symptoms that are additional to the diagnostic criteria for depression that a patient has already met.

The symptoms of atypical depression are opposite those typically associated with depression. Symptoms tend to be chronic and usually begin in adolescence. Rather than eating and sleeping less, people with atypical depression eat and sleep more. They often experience prolonged fatigue, but they can still experience emotional reactivity to things, whereas people with major depression often do not experience strong emotional reactivity to life events. Additionally, people with this form of depression tend to be extraordinarily sensitive to perceived or actual rejection from other people.

## SEASONAL AFFECTIVE DISORDER

Seasonal affective disorder seems to be related to seasonal changes in sunlight. People who suffer from this disorder typically become depressed in the fall and winter when the hours of daylight reduce, and they begin to feel better in the spring. During fall and winter, they experience symptoms similar to those of atypical depression. Individuals with seasonal affective disorder tend to feel fatigued, sleep excessively, and have an increased appetite, especially for

Light therapy is believed to be an effective treatment for people who suffer from seasonal affective disorder, especially if they are unable to spend significant time outdoors during daylight hours.

sugary, salty, and fatty foods. Some researchers believe that the reduced sunlight in late fall causes a change in brain chemistry, which leads to depression. The treatment that seems to be most effective is surprisingly simple—sitting in front of a brightly lit box for about thirty minutes each day during the winter months. Proper light boxes emit high intensity light and are designed for people who suffer from seasonal affective disorder. Mood, energy level, and concentration seem to improve as a result of light therapy. These light boxes can be purchased online or obtained from a medical professional. In some severe cases, antidepressant medication or talk therapy are sometimes combined with the light therapy for more effective treatment.

## POSTPARTUM DEPRESSION

The term *postpartum* comes from the prefix *post* (after) and the word *parturition* (the process of giving birth). Many people experience symptoms of depression after giving birth. About 15 percent of birth parents display the symptoms of major depression—insomnia, loss of appetite, and inability to function—with a focus on the baby and parenthood. Postpartum depression is the result of the hormonal changes associated with giving birth and the stress that comes with having a child. People who suffer from this type of depression often fixate on the fear that they are bad parents who are unable to care for their babies. Without treatment, this condition can have a negative effect on a parent's relationship with their child and they may not be able to bond with the baby. Additionally, people who give birth and put the baby up for adoption may still experience postpartum depression.

In severe cases of postpartum depression, the depression can progress into psychosis, with the parent experiencing thoughts and feelings of wanting to harm themselves or their child. This is a treatable medical condition, and people should seek help from their doctor, family members, or friends, depending on the severity of their distress. However, a person experiencing thoughts and feelings of wanting to hurt themselves or their child must take themselves and their child to the emergency department as soon as possible to prevent harm.

## DEPRESSION WITH PSYCHOTIC FEATURES

Psychosis is a mental state where a person experiences hallucinations (seeing or hearing things that aren't really there) or delusions (irrational thoughts or fears) that are not in line with reality. Someone experiencing a psychotic episode is unable to distinguish their hallucinations or delusions from the things that are happening in the real world. Depression with psychotic features is severe depression accompanied by symptoms of psychosis. These symptoms include hallucinations and delusions, often in addition to paranoia. People experiencing psychosis may hear distressing "voices," which are often suicidal or homicidal. Depression with psychotic features is sometimes related to brain injury.

# SIGNS AND SYMPTOMS

## More than a Case of "the Blues"

When we think of depression, we tend to think of people who express sadness. However, the symptoms of depression may not involve any of the emotions we associate with sadness, and not all people who appear unhappy are suffering from depression. Everyone feels sad, disappointed, and hopeless from time to time. But many people are eventually able to turn away from the sadness and begin to focus on the people and events in their lives that bring them joy. They bounce back from the disappointment and return to the lifestyle and mood they experienced before the disappointment occurred.

For individuals who suffer from depression, however, bouncing back is difficult and sometimes impossible. They find it hard to move on after an event that caused them grief. Little if anything thereafter seems to feel good to them. They feel trapped in a downward spiral, and there seems to be no way out.

Sometimes it is not just a single event or disappointment that causes sadness. Sometimes it is a thread of constant hardship that weaves its way through each day and eventually takes a toll on the individual experiencing it. Teasing or rejection by classmates is one example. Facing houselessness or racism are others. For teenagers who face these kinds of ongoing challenges, every day can be miserable. After facing hardship day after day for a long time, the stress can build up to the point at which some young people become clinically depressed.

Once depression sets in, it changes the way a person thinks. It alters and distorts the person's perceived reality. Life tends to begin feeling gloomy and dull, and the future appears darker. Negative thoughts and pessimism creep in to make it seem that things are bound to go wrong. Feelings of helplessness often take over and make it seem pointless to try to improve things. Self-confidence and self-esteem seem to vanish, and self-blame tends to emerge. It is difficult to remember feeling happy, and it seems impossible to feel hopeful that one will ever feel joy.

What does all of this add up to for teenagers? Some end up developing self-destructive behavior, such as lying, stealing, fighting, skipping school, running away from home, using drugs and alcohol, taking sexual risks, or engaging in self-harm. Some teens attempt or follow through with suicide.

## Features of Depression

When a mental health professional evaluates someone for depression, they look for the presence of two types of symptoms: psychological (mental or emotional) and biological (physical).

Psychological symptoms include:

- Feeling sad, irritable, frustrated, or angry
- Experiencing a loss of interest in most activities that were once enjoyable
- Having difficulty thinking, concentrating, or making decisions
- Feeling worthless or guilty
- Having repeated thoughts of death or suicide
- Experiencing psychosis

Biological symptoms include:

- Experiencing a change in appetite and significant increase or decrease in weight
- Having difficulty falling asleep and staying asleep at night, or sleeping too much
- Feeling restless or fidgety, or experiencing slowed movements
- Feeling tired and lacking energy
- Experiencing unexplained physical ailments such as headaches

Receiving a depression diagnosis means that an individual is experiencing at least five of these symptoms, with at least one symptom consisting of low or depressed mood, and that the symptoms have been present for at least two weeks and interfere with daily activities.

## PSYCHOLOGICAL SYMPTOMS

Feeling sad, not being able to smile, and crying over things that ordinarily would not be upsetting are symptoms that some young people experience when they are depressed. But feeling aggressive, cranky, and irritable can be as much a sign of depression as feeling down in the dumps. Many depressed young people feel frustrated for no apparent reason, resulting in angry outbursts, especially at home. The anger can be directed at themselves or at others. Picking fights with family or household members is common. Depressed individuals also often become enveloped in feelings of loneliness and self-pity, potentially leading to thoughts or statements such as "No one likes me" or "Life is unfair" or "Everyone is mean to me."

Comments such as "I'm bored" or "I don't want to do that—it's dumb" or "Why bother—what's the point?" may also signal depression. Many depressed young people lose interest in activities that once gave them pleasure. Some might quit a sports team while others stop taking dance or music lessons. Others decline to participate in social activities with their friends. As a result, many depressed young people end up feeling lonely, which only adds to their depression. Some depressed teenagers lose interest in food and lose weight. Others seem to crave food and never feel satisfied. Foods rich in carbohydrates (cake, cookies, potato chips, and bread, for example) are especially appealing to many of these individuals. Some even hide food to be eaten later.

Paying attention and concentrating on a task are often difficult for depressed young people. Just as their body movements may seem to occur in slow motion, so may their thinking. For example, some may have trouble focusing on a conversation. Many suffer a decline in school performance because of these symptoms. Others

A young person works on a model plane kit. Depressed individuals often lose interest in their hobbies, which can be a sign of their disorder.

have difficulty making decisions, and they may turn to caregivers or other adults for help.

Depression and low self-esteem both intensify each other. Many people who suffer from depression may feel that they are not as capable as other people and that they are incompetent. They tend to downplay their successes but blow their failures out of proportion. They may say things such as, "I can't do anything right" or "I'm stupid." Most are very sensitive to criticism from others. Many blame themselves and put themselves down for things that do not turn out according to plan. They view negative events, no matter how small, as proof of their shortcomings. These feelings also carry over to friendships, and they may believe no one wants to be friends with them.

Some depressed young people become especially preoccupied with death. They may surround themselves with music, magazines, digital media, and computer games that involve death or morbid themes. All young people may engage with this media even if they are not suicidal, but if somebody suddenly becomes obsessed with death when they were not before, this may be a warning sign. Others become obsessed with thoughts of killing themselves and devise a suicide plan.

Some depressed teenagers hear voices that tell them they are bad or worthless. Others experience delusional thinking, which involves incorrect interpretations of reality. Some may experience paranoia, feeling as if people are out to get them or that the world is conspiring against them in some way.

## BIOLOGICAL SYMPTOMS

Many people with depression struggle with sleep. Tossing and turning after going to bed, waking up several times during the night and not being able to fall back to sleep, waking up too early in the morning, and sleeping too much are all problems associated with depression. Feeling tired upon waking, even for those who have had enough sleep, is not uncommon.

Depression can affect the speed at which a person moves. Some individuals become restless and jittery, while others seem to be moving in slow motion. Starting to fidget with clothing or hair more often can be a sign of depression, as can someone sitting idly, giving one-word answers, or speaking in monotone when they usually don't.

Many depressed people feel exhausted. Some can barely find the energy to do much more than lie down. This may lead to family, household members, or friends misunderstanding their

A teenager sleeps during class. Excessive tiredness is a well-known symptom of depression. But any change in someone's sleep patterns, including being unable to sleep well or at all, can also signal the disorder.

situation and thinking that they are lazy or uninterested instead of depressed.

It's important to note that any changes someone experiences are in relation to their normal baseline energy levels. Some people are always more restless or more slow-moving than others. This is okay and does not mean they have depression. But a change in somebody's baseline is when it can become a warning sign.

Stomachaches or headaches that cannot be explained may also signal depression. So may a general sense of not feeling well physically. Some people experiencing depression find themselves making repeated visits to the doctor due to physical pain and discomfort. These ailments may also be the result of feeling anxious about school performance or about being accepted by friends and classmates.

# Coexisting Conditions

More often than not, depression is not the only mental illness that someone is experiencing. If somebody is depressed, they may be dealing with other forms of mental illness or disability, including anxiety disorders, conduct disorder, oppositional defiant disorder, attention deficit hyperactivity disorder, learning disabilities, eating disorders, and substance use disorder. Often when another condition coexists with depression, both must be treated, which makes management of both disorders more difficult.

## ANXIETY DISORDERS

Some of the anxiety disorders that affect teenagers include separation anxiety disorder, generalized anxiety disorder, obsessive-compulsive disorder, phobias, and post-traumatic stress disorder. These conditions often coexist with major depression.

Feeling homesick when away from home, worrying about the well-being of their caregivers, and avoiding going to school are some of the signs of separation anxiety disorder.

A sign of generalized anxiety disorder can be excessively worrying about future events (an upcoming test, for example) and past events, often with feelings of guilt. Young people with this disorder tend to be perfectionists and to care a great deal about what others think of them. They often appear anxious, engaging in nervous movement such as foot tapping or nail-biting. They also tend to be irritable and to become tired easily.

Obsessive-compulsive disorder is characterized by an obsession, which is a persistent thought or impulse to do something, and usually a compulsion, which is a repetitive behavior. However, some people with this disorder solely experience obsessive thinking.

A young person bites their nails. Nail biting, skin picking, and other fidgeting may result from people with anxiety physically expressing their nerves.

Most individuals with obsessive-compulsive disorder experience the thought or impulse and then feel forced to act on it. For example, a person may have obsessive thoughts about coming into contact with germs. As a result, they may feel compelled to wash their hands over and over again in an attempt to rid them of germs.

Phobias are intense and irrational fears of certain objects, activities, or circumstances, such as an excessive fear of heights or enclosed spaces. Some young people suffer from social phobias, such as an excessive fear of speaking in front of the class or eating in front of other people.

Post-traumatic stress disorder can result from experiencing an event that is shocking, unanticipated, and beyond what usually occurs in a person's life. Examples include physical and sexual abuse, sexual assault, kidnapping, and threatened death. When these events happen, the resulting trauma can be so severe that an individual may be left with intense feelings of fear and helplessness.

Symptoms of post-traumatic stress disorder include recurrent and distressing memories or dreams of the event and feeling as if the traumatic event were happening all over again. People suffering from the disorder may feel detached from familiar activities, be irritable and anxious, and experience problems with sleep and concentration. People who witness a trauma to another person or who learn about a trauma that has affected a close friend or family member may also suffer the onset of post-traumatic stress disorder as a result.

## CONDUCT DISORDER

Individuals who suffer from conduct disorder exhibit behavior that ignores the basic rights of other people and breaks the rules of society. They show no remorse for their actions. Many young people with conduct disorder are what other young people at school might think of as bullies. They tend to start fights and to be deliberately cruel to people or animals. They also tend to lie, steal, stay out late at night, run away from home, skip school, and intentionally destroy property. In addition, young people who suffer from conduct disorder often use drugs and alcohol and take sexual risks. This disorder is more commonly diagnosed in boys and men.

## OPPOSITIONAL DEFIANT DISORDER

Individuals who suffer from oppositional defiant disorder exhibit a persistent pattern of negative, hostile, and defiant behavior that lasts for six months or longer. Many young people with this disorder tend to argue and have angry outbursts at home. They are somewhat more obedient and in control of themselves in public places, including school.

It is not unusual for young people with oppositional defiant disorder to tease and torment siblings, provoke shouting matches with their caregivers, and break rules just for spite. Physical fighting may also erupt. Those with oppositional defiant disorder are also known for blaming others for the problems that they face and even for their behaviors. Some individuals with the disorder go on to develop conduct disorder.

## ATTENTION DEFICIT HYPERACTIVITY DISORDER

Finding it difficult to stick with a task, sit still, be patient, and think before acting are all symptoms of attention deficit hyperactivity disorder. Young people with this disorder may be disorganized or inattentive in schoolwork, chores at home, or other daily life. Many

Having a messy or disorganized room does not necessarily mean someone has attention deficit hyperactivity disorder. But many people with this disorder may have trouble staying organized or cleaning up their rooms, backpacks, or other spaces.

are forgetful and often misplace their belongings. Forgetfulness, disorganization, and inattentiveness can also be symptoms of depression. Some of the struggles that people with attention deficit hyperactivity disorder face can contribute to the development of depression.

## LEARNING DISABILITIES

Young people who have learning disabilities are not less intelligent than their peers, but they may have trouble with school achievement in reading, writing, speaking, listening, and/or doing mathematics. One of the most common learning disabilities is dyslexia, a language-communication disorder that causes difficulty with reading and comprehension.

## EATING DISORDERS

Compulsive or binge eating, anorexia nervosa, and bulimia nervosa are eating disorders commonly associated with depression. Some individuals suffer from a blend of both anorexia and bulimia. Cisgender women, or people who were assigned female at birth and identify as women, suffer eating disorders at a higher rate than cisgender men. This is likely due in part to massive social pressure and the role of social media in the rise of objectifying female bodies and promoting unhealthy body standards. However, as clinicians begin to recognize the prevalence of these disorders, more and more cisgender men are being diagnosed with eating disorders as well. Additionally, all transgender people experience eating disorders at a higher rate than cisgender people.

Those who suffer from a compulsive or binge eating (consuming large amounts of food in a short period of time) disorder may become significantly overweight and develop medical conditions associated with significant excess weight, such as insulin resistance, high blood pressure, or musculoskeletal disease.

Anorexia nervosa is a sharp decrease in the intake of food or refusal to eat at all. Although someone with anorexia will often be at or below a body weight that is considered average for their age and build, they continue to see themselves as fat. Other symptoms include developing unusual eating habits, exercising obsessively, and a halting of monthly menstrual periods due to low body weight.

Bulimia nervosa involves binge eating and then purging (getting rid of the food) by vomiting, by using laxatives or diuretics to cause bowel movements, or by exercising excessively. Other symptoms include developing eating rituals, eating secretly, and spending long periods of time in the bathroom, especially after eating. Someone with bulimia tends to suffer from low self-esteem and be overly concerned with the opinions of other people.

## ALCOHOL AND DRUG ABUSE

Depression is a leading cause of alcohol and substance use disorders. Many individuals who suffer from depression are in such deep emotional pain that they attempt to self-medicate with alcohol or drugs to escape sad or lonely feelings or to feel less anxious. In addition to alcohol and cigarettes, teenagers may use marijuana, LSD, cocaine, heroin, and other drugs. Some inhale the gas in aerosol cans of glue, paint, room deodorizers, and whipped cream to get high, which is very dangerous.

Both alcohol and drugs may numb the pain and relieve feelings of anxiety—but these effects are only temporary and do nothing to fix the root cause of depression. After the effects of these substances wear off, the depression returns and can even intensify after substance use.

Smoking, vaping, and other drug and alcohol use may result from people with depression trying to escape or relieve negative feelings. But the effects of these substances can be dangerous or worsen people's depression.

Depending on the substance, the negative effects of substance use can include memory loss, infections, increased risk of psychosis, lung disease, risk-taking behavior, accidents, school failure, and in the long term, organ failure or even death. Just as with depression, there are many treatments available for substance abuse such as structured rehabilitation programs, support groups, and medications.

# CHAPTER THREE

# DIAGNOSIS AND TREATMENT

## Diagnosis

Doctors can diagnose some conditions with a blood test or X-ray. This is not so with depression. Diagnosing depression is a complex process. Health professionals must gather information from a variety of sources. Then a health professional experienced in diagnosing and treating depression must analyze it.

Psychiatrists are medical doctors and can prescribe medication. Some psychiatrists provide psychotherapy (talk therapy), while others leave this to psychologists. Psychologists typically hold either a PhD (doctor of philosophy) or a PsyD (doctor of psychology) degree. They are not medical doctors, so they cannot prescribe medication. Their training mainly focuses on talk therapy to change thought and behavior patterns. Psychiatrists and psychologists

Universities, medical centers, and other places with mental health clinics usually have several different services available. Their staff can help identify what services a person needs and which therapist might be the best fit for them.

sometimes work together in diagnosing and treating a patient with depression.

A pediatrician, a family physician, a school psychologist, or a guidance counselor can recommend qualified mental health professionals who specialize in working with teenagers. Universities, hospitals, and medical centers have mental health professionals on staff. Many universities have a psychology department with an in-house clinic, and most medical schools and medical centers have private practice groups or mental health clinics.

More than one health professional may have to take part in the evaluation process since it is complex. The process should include a physical examination, patient history, psychological testing, and an interview with the teenager as well as with their caregivers. Because depression tends to affect so many aspects of a young person's life, the mental health professional making the diagnosis must find out how the young person is functioning in all areas of their life.

## PHYSICAL EXAMINATION

The symptoms of depression frequently involve physical discomfort, such as stomachaches, headaches, fatigue, and changes in appetite. A pediatrician or family physician is often the first health professional that caregivers and teens turn to in order to figure out what is going on. The doctor will do a thorough physical examination to determine whether there is another condition causing the symptoms. Other conditions such as diabetes, thyroid problems, and the viral illness mononucleosis can be associated with stomach discomfort, weight changes, mood changes, or fatigue. The doctor may also order blood and urine laboratory tests and possibly an electrocardiogram, a test that checks the electrical activity of the heart, to gather as much information as possible.

If the results of the physical examination and tests show no problems, and if the doctor still suspects that depression exists, they will likely suggest consulting a mental health professional. The doctor can recommend psychiatrists and psychologists in the area, especially those who specialize in evaluating teenagers. One of these mental health professionals should conduct the rest of the evaluation.

## PATIENT HISTORY

The psychiatrist or the psychologist will gather information from the teenager's caregivers to find out about the teenager's history. This history includes developmental information such as the age at which they began to crawl, walk, and talk, and medical information, including any illnesses, accidents, and surgeries that have occurred since infancy. The doctor will ask about the adolescent's psychological background, including their temperament and fears they've had since early childhood. They will also ask about their educational history, including their school performance and whether they have trouble paying attention. The caregivers will provide details about the teenager's family, including the relationship between caregivers or other household members. They will also note any mood or anxiety disorders, learning disabilities, or alcoholism in biological relatives.

## PSYCHOLOGICAL TESTS

Mental health professionals use many different tests and questionnaires to assess an individual's attention span, impulsiveness, and self-esteem. Other tests reveal the person's self-image, social issues, or moodiness. They may also assess a patient's baseline personality, habits, and thought patterns. These professionals will often ask caregivers to fill out questionnaires that address how their teenager behaves in various settings, such as home or school.

## INTERVIEWS

The psychiatrist or the psychologist will usually talk with the caregivers and sometimes the other children in the family or household before talking with the teenager. That professional will hear each person's perspective on what problems they deal with at home and will evaluate how the household influences the teenager seeking a diagnosis. The psychiatrist or the psychologist will then meet with the teenager separately to hear their perspective. They will discuss specific symptoms during this meeting.

Before making a diagnosis, the psychiatrist or the psychologist may want to speak with teachers or coaches to learn more about school performance and behavior. This step is not always part of the diagnostic process but can help the professional understand how their patient functions outside the home. Teachers usually have insight into how their students relate to fellow classmates.

After reviewing all the information gathered from the physical examination, patient history, psychological tests, and interviews, the psychiatrist or the psychologist will make a diagnosis. If the patient has depression, the professional will determine both the form of depression and its severity before recommending treatment options. They will also determine whether the patient has any coexisting conditions.

## Coping with the Diagnosis

Some teenagers may feel angry about receiving a depression diagnosis. Others deny that a problem exists, doubting the psychiatrist's or psychologist's findings. Some are frightened, and some might feel ashamed because of beliefs they have about what a diagnosis of depression means or because of perceived social pressures.

Many caregivers go through these same emotions once their child has been diagnosed with depression. Some even feel guilty. They may feel that they are responsible, either genetically or by the way they have raised their child, for causing the depression. But nobody is entirely responsible for somebody else developing depression. Each individual's unique combination of genetics and life experiences combine to either make them susceptible or resistant to depression.

However, most teenagers and their caregivers feel relieved

when they receive a diagnosis and especially when they learn that treatment is available, because it allows them to name what is going on and seek treatment.

Depression causes young people to have trouble taking initiative, developing independence and self-confidence, and establishing their own identity. Even more pressing is the fact that depression can lead to self-harming behavior, including suicide. Consequently, it is important for them to get help as early as possible to prevent episodes from recurring and to foster their personal development. With proper treatment, most young people who suffer from depression can get better.

"Don't be afraid to start the conversation with your primary care physician," advises Dr. Danielle Weitzer, a psychiatry resident at Rowan University School of Osteopathic Medicine. "Depression is one of the most common mental health disorders, [so] fortunately, there [are] effective treatment strategies available. With a physician's guidance, a patient can find the right combination of lifestyle changes and medication for an improved quality of life."

## Treatment

The most common treatment for depression is psychotherapy or a combination of psychotherapy and medication. Although many mental health professionals accept psychotherapy alone as a beneficial treatment method, especially for less severe depression, they usually do not favor using medication without the support of psychotherapy. This is because medication will boost the levels of neurotransmitters, making it easier to form new neural connections and restore proper brain functioning,

The American Psychiatric Association announced changes to its recommendations for depression treatment in 2019. The new guidelines focus on a more personalized approach to treatment for people with depression. Each person's treatment should be tailored to their specific needs, according to the severity of their symptoms and their age. In general, doctors should assess the patient's condition and adjust treatment accordingly. Treatment should include a combination of therapies including medication, psychotherapy, and changes in behavior, such as diet and exercise. Doctors should also monitor patients long-term who have had three prior episodes of depression or suffer from chronic illness, rather than just treating their current depressive episode. Other new recommendations include considering the following treatments:

but it will not solve the problems of coping with stress, feeling more self-confident, or forming friendships, all of which can continue to contribute to poor mental health if not addressed. People can learn the skills needed to overcome these problems in psychotherapy. As a result, for many young people who are mildly or moderately depressed, psychotherapy alone may alleviate the symptoms of depression without the use of medication. But those who are more severely depressed may also need medication.

- New treatments such as transcranial magnetic
  stimulation (electromagnetic stimulation of
  brain regions linked with depression) and vagus
  nerve stimulation (electric charges delivered
  to the vagus nerve, which links the brain to
  internal organs)
- Regular exercise, which has shown proven
  benefits to older people with depression and
  those with other chronic medical problems
- The use of the medicinal plant Saint-John's-wort
  (under medical supervision) in people who are
  unwilling or unable to use psychotherapy or
  pharmacotherapy
- Electroconvulsive therapy (shock therapy), for
  people who do not benefit from medication,
  especially older adults who often have lower
  responses to medication

## Psychotherapy

Psychotherapy is the treatment of a mental or emotional disorder by
a professionally trained and licensed individual who uses a variety
of techniques to improve the mental health and coping skills of a
patient or group of patients. Psychotherapists can be psychologists,
psychiatrists, counselors, or social workers. Psychotherapy is
sometimes called talk therapy.

Through regular meetings (daily, weekly, or monthly, for

A young person meets with a therapist. There are many kinds of therapies, and therapists often specialize in one or more types. But all therapists share the goal of helping people work through their feelings, behaviors, and other parts of their life.

example) with a trained mental health professional, people experiencing depression learn how to make positive changes in their attitude, emotions, and behavior. Some feel better after just talking about their concerns, while others must actively find solutions to problems that contributed to the development of their depression. For example, some people must learn to express anger and hostility without becoming aggressive. Others may have to work on setting appropriate boundaries with people in their life, so that they do not rely on others too much to solve their own problems. In addition, psychotherapy helps people work through the relationship problems that accompany depression. Improving social skills can help in the recovery process and is important in people's general well-being. It can help them find a support system to lean on, or they may be able to connect with others who are experiencing or have experienced depression.

Therapists use several types of psychotherapy to treat their patients. Research suggests that a combination of cognitive therapy and behavioral therapy, called cognitive behavioral therapy, is most effective in treating depression. Other effective types of psychotherapy doctors use to treat depression are interpersonal therapy, family therapy, and group therapy.

## COGNITIVE BEHAVIORAL THERAPY

Cognitive therapy helps change negative and distorted views of the self, the world, and the future. It focuses on changing unhealthy or unhelpful thought patterns and replacing them with constructive, growth-oriented thought patterns. It also helps people learn the skills necessary for coping with emotions and relating to other people. Behavioral therapy focuses on changing specific problem behaviors by using rewards for desirable behavior and either no rewards or negative consequences for undesirable behavior. A combination of these two approaches helps people view themselves and the world more positively and accurately, get involved in activities they enjoy, and interact successfully with other people.

## INTERPERSONAL THERAPY

This therapy helps people identify and solve the problems they are having with other people. For young people, these problems may include not being able to form friendships, being rejected by classmates, or excessive arguing with their caregivers. Interpersonal therapy teaches communication skills that help a person successfully and confidently interact with other people. Whether the relationship problem triggers the depression or whether the depression causes the relationship problem, interpersonal therapy for depression is designed to identify the nature of the problem and then find solutions.

## FAMILY THERAPY

In addition to meeting alone with the teenager, the therapist may also meet with their family. Family therapy not only helps all members of the family understand and cope with depression, but it also investigates the possibility that the young person's depression stems from problems within the family. These could include marital problems between their caregivers, a lack of adequate guidance for the teenager, no set limits, or the absence of a parent or caregiver through divorce or death. The therapist helps all family members learn to communicate more effectively with one another and teaches them ways to solve problems as they arise.

## GROUP THERAPY

Group therapy involves a therapist working with a group of clients. Although some teenagers feel uncomfortable in a group setting with their peers, others actually feel more comfortable. Being in a group where the other people are also experiencing depression can help make the person feel less isolated and alone. In addition, many teenagers are often more willing to accept suggestions and solutions from their peers than from a doctor or a therapist. An added advantage of the group setting is that the participants take turns speaking, so a person speaks only when they want to.

There is no one type of therapy that works best for everyone, and many people find that different types or combinations of

Group therapy can be a good option for people who are uncomfortable in solo therapy or who want to connect with peers with similar experiences.

therapy work better for them at different stages of their lives. Some people even end up completing a therapy course that is a combination or overlap of many different types of therapy.

## CHOOSING A THERAPIST

The therapists who are most likely to successfully help a person experiencing depression are those who provide a trusting environment, are able to establish a comfortable bond with the person, and are able to put the patient and their support system at ease. The better the match between the teenager and the therapist, the more successful the treatment is likely to be. Research has shown that the single greatest factor in the success of psychotherapy is the comfort the patient feels with their therapist.

A therapist may be a psychiatrist, a psychologist, a social worker, or a psychiatric nurse. Many states also have certified counselors. Counselors often have a specialization, such as family or marriage counseling. It is always best to choose a therapist who is licensed in their field. This indicates that they have adequate training and experience in psychotherapy. In addition, licensed therapists must meet professional standards, and they must stay on top of changes and progress in their field by updating their education from time to time.

Finding a therapist for the first time can be challenging. People might struggle to find someone who specializes in their specific needs or who they feel they can relate to. If someone has health insurance, they might prefer to find a therapist who their insurance will pay for. In this case, insurance companies will often provide a list of qualified therapists in your area.

However, there are many other resources to help find a therapist. Many therapists have online profiles that show where they work, what they specialize in, what kinds of education and experience they have, how payment works, and more. Some profiles may even include reviews from former patients. The American Psychological Association offers a Psychologist Locator tool on their website that allows people to search for qualified and licensed therapists in their area. People can also talk to their primary care physician about receiving a referral to a qualified mental health professional.

## Medication

When a patient's depression is severe or has been long-lasting, a mental health professional may prescribe them medication to be used in combination with psychotherapy. Only medical doctors can prescribe medication. Ideally, a psychiatrist experienced in treating depression in teenagers should decide what medication and dosage are best. Pediatricians and family doctors may also prescribe medication, but they are typically not trained specifically in treating depression in teenagers.

Antidepressants are the medications used to treat depression. They can also be used to treat other conditions, including obsessive-compulsive disorder and generalized anxiety disorder. As the medication balances the levels of neurotransmitters in the brain, clearer and more accurate thinking becomes possible. This helps the individual receiving treatment be more receptive to the emotional and behavioral changes that the therapist will strive for during psychotherapy.

Antidepressant medication comes in various types and works in different ways. Although these medications are sometimes thought of as mood elevators, they are really mood regulators. They simply restore the amounts of neurotransmitters in the brain to normal levels.

Antidepressant medications are not "uppers," meaning that they have no mood-altering effect on individuals who are not depressed, and they are not addictive. Different antidepressants work in different ways to correct the amounts of neurotransmitters in the brain. Some slow down the breakdown (destruction) of neurotransmitters, while others prevent the reuptake (reabsorption) of neurotransmitters. And some increase the amount of neurotransmitters released from nerve endings.

Antidepressant medications can be grouped into three main categories: selective serotonin reuptake inhibitors (SSRIs), tricyclic antidepressants, and monoamine oxidase inhibitors (MAOIs). Of them, SSRIs are the most widely prescribed.

# THE EFFECTS OF EXERCISE ON DEPRESSION

"In people who are depressed, neuroscientists have noticed that the hippocampus in the brain—the region that helps regulate mood—is smaller. Exercise supports nerve cell growth in the hippocampus, improving nerve cell connections, which helps relieve depression," explained Dr. Michael Miller, assistant professor of psychiatry at Harvard Medical School.

According to a 2023 study published in the *British Journal of Sports Medicine*, exercise is at least as effective as the standard measures of psychotherapy and medication for treating depression, and by some measures it is even better than these common treatments. The study was the largest study done to date of using exercise to treat depression, pooling studies done at forty-one different institutions with over two thousand participants. It showed that people with depression who exercised at least three days a week improved their depression symptoms significantly, by as many as 6.5 points on some scales for assessing depression. An increase of 3 points is considered clinically significant, or likely to represent an actual change in symptoms.

The exercise interventions studied included walking, running, and weightlifting, among others. This means you may not have to be exercising strenuously or for long periods of time to reap the mental health benefits. Just twenty minutes of moving your body three times a week could have positive effects for your mental health. And the most important thing to remember is that something is better than nothing. Here are some ideas to exercise in a fun way:

- Take your dog, parent, grandparent, or sibling for a walk.
- Put on five of your favorite songs and dance.
- Play basketball with friends.
- Ride a bike.
- Play tag with friends or cousins.
- Play soccer with friends.
- Create an obstacle course in your backyard.
- Jump on a trampoline for twenty minutes.
- Go for a swim in a lake or pool.

For people who don't prefer to exercise alone, exercising with a friend or family member can be a way to receive the mental health benefits of the exercise while connecting with their community.

## SELECTIVE SEROTONIN REUPTAKE INHIBITORS

Fluoxetine (trademark: Prozac), sertraline (Zoloft), escitalopram (Lexapro), and paroxetine (Paxil) are drugs that prevent the reuptake of the neurotransmitter serotonin. Reuptake happens when a neuron reabsorbs a neurotransmitter that it released.  These drugs allow greater amounts of serotonin to remain in the brain, restoring the levels to normal. Researchers have found that Prozac can also help some young people who suffer from anxiety disorders and obsessive-compulsive disorder. SSRIs have few serious side effects and are the most prescribed antidepressants. The most common side effects that seem to be associated with SSRIs are headaches and nausea.

## TRICYCLIC ANTIDEPRESSANTS

Tricyclic antidepressants, such as imipramine (Tofranil) and desipramine (Norpramin), are similar to SSRIs, but they raise the levels of norepinephrine as well as serotonin. Common side effects include dry mouth, constipation, and drowsiness. They sometimes cause increased heart rate, so people with heart conditions cannot take them.

## MONOAMINE OXIDASE INHIBITORS

Monoamine oxidase is an enzyme (a protein produced in a cell) that is found in many parts of the body. In the brain, monoamine oxidase breaks down norepinephrine and serotonin. MAOIs block this breakdown. This allows greater amounts of these neurotransmitters to remain in the brain, restoring their levels to normal. Phenelzine (Nardil), tranylcypromine (Parnate), and isocarboxazid (Marplan) are MAOIs. Monoamine oxidase inhibitors are often prescribed for people who do not respond to tricyclics.

# ANTIDEPRESSANTS DON'T WORK THE WAY MANY PEOPLE THINK THEY DO

Antidepressants, mainly selective serotonin reuptake inhibitors, are the most prescribed medications to treat depression, and they have been shown to be effective. But the most common viewpoint—that these drugs work simply by correcting a "chemical imbalance" in the brain—is not quite correct. If this were true, then we would expect antidepressants to always work, by correcting the chemical imbalance, and to work very quickly, as the chemical modulating effects take place within hours. But antidepressants don't work for everyone, and when they do work, they take at least six weeks to see a significant effect. Why is this?

The current prevailing theory of depression is that chronic stress can cause a loss of neural connections in the brain, which then in turn causes an imbalance of brain chemicals. If correct, this theory means that a chemical imbalance is the symptom, not the cause, of depression. SSRIs, then, would be effective against depression for some people for two reasons. Firstly, they help the brain to make new neural connections, effectively combating the loss that causes many people to become depressed in the first place. Secondly, there is some benefit, known as the placebo effect, that comes simply from taking the medication regardless of what it is doing, because it acts as a reminder that the person is doing something to take care of their own mental health.

One major drawback of MAOIs specifically when compared to other antidepressants is that combining them with certain foods, beverages, and medications can cause a serious— and sometimes fatal—reaction. Patients must avoid foods and beverages that contain large amounts of the amino acid tyramine, including aged cheese, processed meats such as hot dogs and pepperoni, and alcohol including wine and beer. They must also avoid certain drugs, including nasal decongestants and cough medicines. These foods and medicines in combination with MAOIs can cause chest pain, headaches, vomiting, and severely elevated blood pressure. Because some teenagers might have a hard time giving up foods such as pepperoni pizza and hot dogs, and because some drink wine or beer, doctors are reluctant to prescribe MAOIs for them.

## LITHIUM

Doctors prescribe lithium to treat bipolar disorder. It effectively treats both the manic and depressive episodes that are characteristic of this disorder. Researchers are still trying to understand how lithium works. There is a fine line between just the right amount of lithium and too much lithium in the body. Too much lithium could be toxic, so doctors must carefully monitor individuals who take this drug. They also need to do regular blood tests to keep track of the lithium level in the body. Side effects include weight gain, stomach upset, and fatigue. If the patient also experiences hallucinations or delusions, the doctor may prescribe an antipsychotic medication in addition to the lithium to relieve these symptoms. Lithium is one of the only psychiatric medications that has been proven to decrease the risk of suicidal ideation and intent.

## OTHER ANTIDEPRESSANTS

Researchers are always working to develop new medications for
depression. SSRIs such as duloxetine (Cymbalta), venlafaxine
(Effexor), and desvenlafaxine (Pristiq) treat depression by
increasing the amounts of serotonin and norepinephrine,
which help maintain brain chemical balance. Bupropion is a
norepinephrine and dopamine reuptake inhibitor. One form of it,
called Wellbutrin, treats major depressive disorder and seasonal
affective disorder. Some doctors prescribe another form,
Zyban, to help people stop smoking. It can reduce cravings and
other withdrawal effects. Trazodone (Desyrel) and mirtazapine
(Remeron) are antidepressants that also have calming effects.
Patients take these medications in the evening to treat their
depression and to help them sleep.

## RESPONSE TO MEDICATION

Everyone responds differently to medication. What works for one
person may not work for another. It is important to let a doctor help
decide whether the medication is effective or whether another one
would be more effective. Many doctors find that a combination of
medications works best.

Antidepressant medication becomes effective gradually, and
it must be taken continuously to work. It typically takes between
four and six weeks before the medication becomes effective, and
full relief from symptoms may take months. The doctor may have a
patient try more than one medication before settling on the best one
and the proper dosage. This can sometimes take several months.
It is often difficult to be patient during this long wait. Some young
people want to give up and just stop taking the medication, but
sticking with it can pay off in the long run.

It may take a long time to find the right antidepressants and for the medication to start working. Some people also have to switch dosages or medications later if their response to the medication changes. But many people with depression find the benefits to be worth the wait.

Some of the positive results include being better able to concentrate, think through and make decisions, and cope with life's disappointments. Patients taking the proper medication can expect a return to their baseline appetite and sleep patterns. Perhaps the most welcome change is the change that people can find with their relationships. Because anxiety and irritability tend to fade when the levels of neurotransmitters in the brain are boosted, people who take a medication that works for them may find it easier to build relationships with people and spend time with their loved ones.

# Electroconvulsive Therapy

In rare instances, someone's depression is so severe that a combination of psychotherapy and medication is not effective. In those cases, the doctor may prescribe brain stimulation therapy, a type of therapy in which electricity is applied to activate or inhibit the brain.

Electroconvulsive therapy involves passing an electrical current through the brain two or three times per week for six to twelve weeks. Because of its history and portrayal in media, many people worry that this therapy, commonly called shock therapy, is dangerous.

Modern electroconvulsive therapy is safer and very different than the electroshock therapy of the past. When the treatment was first introduced in the late 1930s, patients were awake during the procedure, and the shocks were often painful. But modern doctors use sedatives and muscle relaxers so the patient feels no pain or discomfort during the treatments. They also monitor the patient's brain waves and vital signs to ensure the patient's safety. When doctors correctly perform modern electroconvulsive therapy, the patient should just feel as if they went to sleep and woke back up again, with no pain.

Electroconvulsive therapy is sometimes used to treat suicidal patients whose lives are in immediate danger. It is also effective for people on medications that interact poorly with antidepressants, for older adults who often have a poorer response to medication, and for people that are currently pregnant and do not want to use other medications. People who receive this therapy are typically treated with psychotherapy and medication following the treatments.

# THE FACTS ABOUT DEPRESSION AND ITS TREATMENT

Getting past the stigma associated with depression and seeking help is the first step toward recovery. The following are common myths about depression and the facts that dispute them.

**Myth:** Depression is not a real medical problem.

**Fact:** Research has proven that depression is a real and serious condition. The medical community acknowledges it is a debilitating disease.

**Myth:** Depression is something that strong people can "snap out of" by thinking positively.

**Fact:** No one chooses to be depressed. People with depression cannot just "snap out of" their condition any more than someone with any other medical condition can.

**Myth:** Depression will just go away on its own.

**Fact:** While depression sometimes goes away without treatment, this is not usually the case. Without treatment, symptoms of depression can continue for weeks, months, or even years.

**Myth:** Antidepressants will make you an "emotionless robot."

**Fact:** Antidepressants are designed to change only the chemicals in your brain that cause the symptoms of depression. They do not to change your ability to experience feelings and interact with daily life, but they can reduce the intensity of negative feelings and help people with depression cope with daily life.

# Hospitalization

When a person suffering from depression has made a suicide attempt, when they have a definite plan for carrying out a suicide, or when they are threatening self-harm or harm to others, hospitalization may be necessary. People who lie in bed all day, stay up all night without being able to sleep, or dissolve into uncontrollable crying spells may also need hospitalization. Anybody who is experiencing psychosis should also consider hospitalization. Hospitalization can also help people who abuse alcohol and drugs to get the help they need.

Hospital settings are controlled, and many inpatient programs offer resources such as counseling, treatment plans, and scheduled medication and therapy. Some people find the hospital to be a good break from the turmoil of family conflict, physical or sexual abuse, pressures at home or school, or humiliation by peers. The therapy included in an inpatient treatment plan usually focuses on helping people find ways to deal with stress and painful feelings.

But hospitalization is not a positive experience for everyone. Some find it more stressful than their lives at home, and they feel greater despair and hopelessness as a result. Consequently, a doctor and anyone else involved should carefully weigh the decision to hospitalize a patient, especially if it is against the patient's wishes.

# How Long Should Treatment Continue?

The mental health professionals involved in a patient's treatment determine its duration. This varies from person to person. It can

People share a meal together. It can be difficult to tell whether someone has depression, and how depression is experienced varies between individuals. But with the right treatment and support, anyone with depression can lead a fulfilling life regardless of their treatment needs and the severity of their disorder.

range from a few weeks to a lifetime, depending on the nature of the depression and its severity. For example, someone with mild depression may emerge from a depressive episode after a few weekly psychotherapy sessions. But someone with bipolar disorder may need treatment with psychotherapy and medication for life. Research has shown that some people who receive treatment for depression overcome the depression and never need treatment again. Others overcome the depression but experience another episode later in life. Still others require treatment on a long-term basis.

# CHAPTER FOUR

# SUICIDE AND ITS PREVENTION

Suicide is the most feared outcome of depression. There has been and continues to be a stigma around this act. Some may feel that a person who committed suicide took the easy way out or that they couldn't see anything to live for. In some cultures and religions, suicide is seen as the ultimate sin and a dishonor. In reality, suicide and thoughts of it are known complications of depression. Wanting to, thinking about, or trying to commit suicide are features of this and other mental illnesses and do not have any bearing on the morality or emotional strength of the person suffering.

Suicide can be a response to depression triggers, such as feelings of loneliness, frustration, and helplessness. It is the third leading cause of death among teenagers in the United States. Only death by accident and homicide claim more teenage lives. And experts believe that some of the deaths that occur in accidents (such as car accidents) each year are really suicides. When someone is the only person in a car at the time of an accident and only that car is involved in the accident (such as when it hits a tree or a telephone pole), there is no way to know for certain whether the event was just an accident or whether the driver really meant to kill themselves.

Teenagers who attempt suicide may display the behaviors discussed later in this chapter, or they may show no warning signs at all. There is no sure way to know who will attempt suicide and who will not. Some people may worry that asking a friend if they are going to commit suicide might "put the idea in their head" and cause someone to do something they otherwise might not have done. However, this has been shown to be untrue. Asking somebody about

A young person meets with a guidance counselor at school. If someone is struggling with their mental health or experiencing suicidal thoughts or behaviors—or knows someone else who is—a school counselor, a teacher, or another trusted adult can help them.

suicidal thoughts or behaviors has not been shown to increase the risk of them committing suicide in the future. If you are worried that someone you know may be contemplating suicide, you can ask them or tell a trusted adult. If you are considering suicide, you can talk to a trusted adult such as a doctor, guidance counselor, or family member. In the US, you can call the suicide hotline by dialing 988. Or you can get to the emergency room as quickly as possible by either driving yourself, asking someone to take you, or calling 911. All of these are ways to get help.

## The Warning Signs of Suicide

The following are signs associated with increased risk of suicide:

- Experiencing a sudden change in personality, such as becoming sadder and more withdrawn or more irritable and explosive
- Suddenly becoming more upbeat and cheerful after being down for a long time
- Experiencing a drop in school performance
- Withdrawing from family, friends, or usual activities
- Neglecting personal appearance, such as not changing clothing from day to day or not combing hair
- Having accidents or engaging in risk-taking behavior, such as driving too fast, running away from home, or using drugs or alcohol
- Expressing strong feelings of worthlessness, such as saying "I'm no good" or "I'm a failure"
- Giving away or throwing away favorite possessions
- Being consumed by the theme of death in books and

magazines, music, computer games, or online

- Talking about life not being worth living, mentioning that they will not be a problem to anyone much longer, or saying "I'm going to kill myself." No mention of suicide should ever be taken lightly. Most teens who attempt suicide speak of their intention beforehand.
- Gathering guns, ropes, or other tools that can be used in carrying out a suicide
- Having made prior suicide attempts

## Depression and Suicide

Depression is one of the biggest risk factors for suicide. Although not every person who suffers from depression attempts suicide, most suicide attempts and completed suicides are carried out by people suffering from depression. About two thirds of people who commit suicide are depressed at the time of their death, and the lifetime suicide risk among patients with untreated depression is about 20 percent. Approximately 15 percent of the people who are depressed commit suicide as a result of their depression.

Along with the rate of depression, the rates of both completed suicides and suicide attempts have risen since 2011. Nearly 20 percent of high schoolers have had serious thoughts of suicide and about 9 percent of high schoolers have made an attempt to commit suicide, according to the National Alliance on Mental Illness. Teens who have been assigned female at birth outnumber teens who have been assigned male at birth in attempted suicides, but those who have been assigned male at birth have the highest rate of completed

Young people celebrating LGBTQ+ pride. The LGBTQ+ community faces a high risk of mental health disorders and suicide. Being able to find or create safe community spaces can help reduce the stress LGBTQ+ people face.

suicides. This is because this group is more likely to choose more violent and final methods, such as gunfire, jumping from a tall height, or hanging.

The group at highest risk for suicide as teens, however, are LGBTQ+ youth. The Trevor Project has published statistics that show that almost half of LGBTQ+ youth seriously considered attempting suicide in 2021. Within the LGBTQ+ community, the highest risk group is transgender and nonbinary youth, as approximately 20 percent of them attempted suicide in 2021. This group is at highest risk due to social and political pressure—rates of depression and suicide have risen as there have been more legislative actions to further marginalize these teens and take away their rights.

Additionally, hate crimes against LGBTQ+ people are on the rise. This also contributes to the social pressures, feelings of being unsafe, and increased risk of suicide they face.

Some teenagers commit suicide without warning, but most speak or at least hint about their suicidal thoughts before an attempt. Any mention of suicide should be taken seriously. Although not every teenager who mentions suicide goes through with the act, most who do have spoken about their feelings or intentions with someone else. Of the individuals who have carried out a suicide or a suicide attempt, many spent time thinking through how they would do it and devised a plan.

## Risk Factors for Suicidal Behavior

Although not all depressed teenagers turn to suicide, some feel that suicide is the only way to end the pain from which they are suffering. Many factors increase the likelihood of a teenager turning to suicide. These include having a family history of suicide or making a previous suicide attempt. It may also include conflict in the home, stressful life events such as moving or academic failure, or feeling rejected by peers. Additionally, personality traits such as perfectionism and impulsiveness, environmental factors such as proximity to guns, and the use of drugs or alcohol can increase someone's risk of suicide compared to their peers who are not dealing with these factors.

Suicide tends to run in biological families. Teenagers who have a close relative, especially a parent, who has committed suicide are more likely to attempt suicide. Scientists believe that genetic abnormalities in the way brain chemicals are produced and used explain part of the reason some individuals engage in suicidal behavior. However, suicidal behavior probably results from a combination of both genetic vulnerability and life events.

Many teenagers who have attempted suicide in the past attempt it again. Although the previous attempt or attempts may not seem serious because they did not succeed, any suicide attempt regardless of severity or outcome should be taken seriously. The next attempt may be fatal.

Young people who steal, have uncontrollable rage, or engage in dangerous behavior are at greater risk for suicide. Some caregivers may react harshly to their teen's behavior, instead of trying to meet the teen where they are at. A teenager who is already vulnerable may see this harsh reaction as proof that their family does not want them around, and this may push them further down the path to suicide.

Traumatic events, such as losing a parent through death, divorce, or abandonment or being physically, sexually, or emotionally abused, can create enough stress to push vulnerable young people to consider suicide.

Some individuals use a suicide attempt to try to get attention or sympathy from a specific person (such as a parent or a romantic partner). Or they may be trying to punish this person for something hurtful they have done. These suicide attempts may sometimes be termed "a cry for help." However, it is important to remember that any suicide attempt, regardless of the motivation or outcome, is a serious event and often an indication of depression or other mental health conditions. People who are mentally well do not attempt suicide. Anybody who has attempted or even considered suicide should seek a psychiatric evaluation and should try to find a strong support system so that they can get the help they need.

Teenagers who live in households where family or household

members argue or communicate poorly, where a parent or caregiver abuses alcohol or other substances, or where caregivers are preoccupied with their own lives also tend to face a greater risk of suicide. Sometimes teens that come from blended families may struggle with inter-family relationships or conflict, which can increase feelings of loneliness or frustration.  If a teenager tries to discuss hopeless or suicidal feelings and their caregivers either ignore them or play down the importance of what they are saying, teenagers are likely to feel even more frustrated and alone. This can increase the risk of suicide.

Because of the way the adolescent brain develops, teenagers tend to be more sensitive to social pressures such as feeling like they are part of a group and avoiding social rejection. When those who are already at risk for committing suicide face experiences that cause them to feel put down or rejected by others, suicide or a suicide attempt is sometimes the outcome. Events that tend to cause teenagers to feel this way include being teased by classmates, having a major argument with their caregivers, being broken up with by a romantic partner, not being chosen as a member of a team or organization, being disciplined at school, and facing problems related to sex and sexuality.

Teenagers who attempt or complete suicide often drink or use drugs just before carrying out the act. Alcohol and drugs tend to make people feel more uninhibited, often increasing feelings of anger and aggression or prompting more risk-taking and self-destructive behavior. In addition, alcohol is a depressant. Although it creates an initial feeling of well-being for some people, it can lead to deeper feelings of depression.

Depressed teenagers tend to have greater difficulty forming and keeping friendships, and many isolate themselves from their peers.

As a result, depressed teenagers often lack a support system when times are particularly tough. Not having a group of caring friends to turn to when life events are painful can add to a young person's despair. Additionally, depressed teenagers are sometimes drawn to others who also have problems, either personally or within their families or households. It is not unusual for these teenagers to support negative and dangerous behavior in one another.

If teens are struggling with finding a supportive community, counselors or other adults may be able to offer advice. Additionally, there are many resources such as support groups, both online and in person, that are available for teens who are looking for community.

Young people who commit suicide often do it on impulse. Having access to guns, either in their own homes or in friends' homes, can make killing themselves all the easier. In fact, after having a previous history of a suicide attempt, having access to a firearm is the number one risk factor for completing suicide for all ages.

Sexual activity and exploring sexual identity can greatly impact young people. Sexually transmitted infections and unwanted pregnancies are some of the physical problems that teens might face. Regarding identity, LGBTQ+ youth grapple with depression at a higher rate than any other teen group. The struggle to determine, understand, and express their sexual, romantic, and gender identities can be difficult in and of itself. This difficulty can become much harder if they do not feel that their families, peers, or communities love and accept them for who they are. These compounding struggles and social pressures put LGBTQ+ youth at the greatest risk for suicide.

Some teenagers cannot tolerate any failure at school. For them, even minor academic failures or disappointments are intolerable. For others, learning disabilities stand in the way of the academic achievement they seek and can lead to criticism from teachers and teasing from classmates. Still others consider it a personal crisis when they face disciplinary action, such as getting detention or being suspended from school.

Teenagers who demand perfection from themselves may turn to suicide when facing disappointments such as losing a competition, not getting into a certain college, or not gaining acceptance through an organization, club, or team.

Teenagers who tend to react impulsively may turn to suicide as a spur-of-the moment response to a problem. This may occur even when the problem is minor, such as having an argument with a friend or facing a disappointment in sports. If someone is already struggling with depression or suicidal ideation, an argument with a friend or a failing grade may be the final straw.

Hearing voices, seeing visions that are not real, or having thoughts that are irrational can lead to suicidal behavior in some teenagers. For some, the voices tell them to kill themselves. This can happen due to alcohol or drug use, or due to an underlying mental illness, such as depression with psychotic features, bipolar disorder, or schizophrenia.

## How Does Suicide Affect Family and Friends?

When a teenager commits suicide, their family and friends are left with deep feelings of grief, anger, and confusion. It can be very difficult for them to come to terms with why it happened. Most feel extremely guilty about not having been able to prevent such a tragedy. Many feel remorse over unresolved issues. They may also feel that the suicide victim has let them down.

When a young person makes a suicide attempt but does not die, it is still common for their family and friends to blame themselves for the attempt. Others feel angry, believing that the teenager could have chosen a different solution. Some family members feel ashamed. They feel that the suicide attempt reflects poorly on the family. And most loved ones feel scared. They wonder when and whether the teenager will make another attempt.

There is no right or wrong way for people to feel after a loved one commits or attempts suicide. It is very emotional and scary and affects everyone involved. Some responses, however, are more effective than others at preventing further attempts.

## What Can Be Done When a Teenager Is Suicidal?

Anyone who shows the warning signs of suicide needs immediate professional help. To wait and see if things improve can have disastrous consequences. In fact, many suicides take place at home while other family or household members are also there. If the individual who is showing suicidal tendencies is already in therapy, someone should contact their therapist immediately. If not, an appointment should be made to see a mental health professional the same day. In the meantime, the individual can call the national Suicide and Crisis Lifeline at 988. If there seems to be immediate danger of the young person harming themselves or others, a call should be placed to emergency services (911 in the US) or the person should be taken immediately to the emergency department.

Most of all, teenagers who are at risk for suicide need a caring person to show concern for their well-being. They need other people to be open and direct with them. It is best to ask a teenager directly about any suicide plans they have made. Experts have learned that talking about a suicide does not put ideas in a young person's head. If an individual is suicidal, the thoughts are already there. The benefit of asking a teenager about their suicidal feelings is that they are likely to feel relieved that someone cares. They may feel more open to discussing the problem and finding alternatives to suicide.

It is important for adults to assure the young person that they care about their safety. The following are additional ways that a parent or other caring adult can help a teenager who has considered suicide:

- Encourage a discussion of the struggles or disappointments that cause their despair.
- Help find other possible ways to solve the problem.
- Share stories of struggles or frustrations the adult faced as a teenager.
- Let them know that depression and other mental health conditions are not from weakness or lack of willpower, but they are serious illnesses that can be treated.
- Let them know that with treatment, they can get better.

Siblings and friends should never agree to keep suicidal thoughts or attempts secret for someone. Whenever a teen mentions suicidal thoughts, their siblings or friends must tell an adult so the teen can seek help as quickly as possible. The suicidal teenager should never be left alone. In addition, caregivers or other responsible adults should lock away any instrument that could

People comfort their friend. When someone is struggling with their mental health, their friends can help by listening to them, comforting them, and contacting a trusted adult if there is ever an emergency situation such as a suicide risk or attempt.

be used to carry out a suicide. These include guns, knives, rope, medications, cleaning solutions, and even the car keys.

Some suicides take place after treatment has begun and the depressed teenager starts to feel better. Family or household members and friends must be alert and watchful even after the danger seems to have passed. Their care and attention help the young person know they have supporters to carry them through their crisis and that they'll eventually be able to get better. With proper treatment and the support of others, teenagers who are suicidal can look ahead to a bright future.

# FAMILY, FRIENDS, AND SCHOOL

Research indicates that having a social support system made up of relationships that involve good communication and trust can help prevent depression, even in individuals who have a family history of the disorder. But when depression does take hold, it powerfully impacts the relationships that individuals have with their family members and their peers. It also often negatively affects their performance at school and at extracurriculars or other activities.

People who are depressed tend to have less social support than people who are not depressed. Is this because the symptoms of depression interfere with a person's ability to form close relationships, or is it because not forming close relationships can result in a vulnerable person developing depression? Both situations can be true.

# Depression and the Family

Most teenagers rely on their caregivers to love and nurture them and to teach them values. But the teenage years are a time of change for young people as well as their parents or caregivers. Although teenagers still rely on their caregivers for guidance, most also feel the need to become more independent. Caregivers, meanwhile, try to adjust to this change. Some struggle with this, while others view it as the natural evolution of their relationship.

Parents or caregivers can sometimes react to their children in ways that injure their children's self-esteem. This can lead to depression in young people. Some caregivers are overly critical of their children and focus on their children's weaknesses rather than their strengths. Others are so preoccupied with their own lives or problems that they do not pay attention to their children's needs. They may also neglect their responsibility to provide guidance.

Some adults physically, sexually, or emotionally abuse the children in their households. Others are absent from the home because of divorce, business travel, or military assignment, which can create a deep sense of loss in their children.

When a parent or caregiver is depressed, family relationships and communication become especially strained. Many depressed caregivers are irritable and impatient when dealing with their children. Some are cold and withdrawn, withholding affection and neglecting their children's needs. Others struggle to participate in family life. Their sad mood and fatigue may make it impossible for them to take part in family activities, help their children develop friendships, or set guidelines for them.

In some cases, the child must take on a parental role. This often happens when someone's parents or caregivers are ill or absent

Since it can be difficult for depressed caregivers to engage or be patient with their children or other family members, they may become stressed, withdrawn, or overwhelmed while spending time with their family.

or when they are emotionally immature and unable to fulfill an appropriate adult role. Even though they strive for independence, teenagers still need to rely on their caregivers from time to time. When a teenager is the caretaker of a parent or other family members, the stress can be overwhelming.

It is not unusual for children of a depressed parent to develop depression themselves, partly because of the hereditary nature of depression and partly because of the everyday stress they must endure at home. Many feel guilty or responsible that their parent is depressed. Others try to protect the parent by holding their own feelings inside. Some resort to negative behavior to get the parent to show a response, or they rebel against the parent's problem.

## HOW A TEENAGER'S DEPRESSION AFFECTS PARENTS AND CAREGIVERS

Parents and caregivers go through a range of emotions when their child is depressed. Many feel confused about why their child has these problems, and they worry about what the future holds. Some feel guilty about their child's problems and blame themselves for being bad caretakers. Most feel deep pain over the feelings of worthlessness and despair that their teenager is suffering.

It is not unusual for depressed young people to be able to control themselves in public settings such as school, only to fall apart at home. Mornings and evenings tend to be more difficult. Waking up in a foul mood and taking too long to get ready for school usually causes an argument with parents or caregivers. And avoiding homework in the evening can lead to anger and frustration. Teenagers who suffer from depression may complain a lot and pick fights with their siblings. It's important to remember that irritability is a symptom of depression, and that it is not the person's fault that they feel this way. They have a mental illness that needs treatment.

At the other end of the spectrum are the teenagers who totally withdraw from their family or household members. Upon returning home from school, they may go directly to their rooms. They may avoid interacting with everyone in the house or at meals.

## HOW A TEENAGER'S DEPRESSION AFFECTS SIBLINGS

The siblings of depressed teenagers often suffer too. Many do not know enough about depression to understand what's wrong. Some worry that they somehow caused their sibling to become depressed. Others feel resentful of the extra time and attention their parents or caregivers devote to the depressed sibling. Still others worry that they, too, may become depressed. And there are some young people who are confused by their sibling's behavior, whether it is marked by irritability or sadness.

## HOW A TEENAGER'S DEPRESSION AFFECTS FRIENDS

The symptoms of depression often interfere with a teenager's ability to make and keep friends. Peers are not likely to respond well to a teenager who does not want to participate in activities and has difficulty concentrating and remembering things. When depressed teenagers continually express negative feelings such as "Nothing ever works out right for me" or "I'm a failure" or "There's no use in even trying," their peers are likely to keep their distance. Their peers might not understand how to comfort them, or they may not relate to what the depressed person is saying. Some depressed teenagers are also argumentative and explosive. The result is that depressed young people may end up with fewer and fewer friends, and some end up with no friends at all.

But other depressed teenagers end up in the opposite situation. They maintain an extremely close relationship with one friend or with a group of friends. Many times these friends also suffer from depression or other problems with their emotions and behavior. The problems they share seem to pull these young people together. They feel a strong desire to spend as much time as possible with one another, often shutting out family and other people. This can be unhealthy when the friends are only reinforcing each other's unhealthy thoughts and behaviors.

# Depression and School

Teenagers who suffer from depression are likely to struggle academically. The symptoms of sadness, hopelessness, fatigue, poor concentration, difficulty remembering, and lack of enthusiasm for participating in activities frequently weaken the person's school performance. For many, having difficulty sleeping and eating and the physical pain of stomachaches or headaches make doing well in school even more difficult. If other conditions coexist with the depression, such as learning disabilities or attention deficit hyperactivity disorder, the situation may become even worse. Many teenagers may behave disruptively as their frustration over their difficulty with schoolwork increases. Then teachers are likely to punish them. As the self-esteem of these young people plummets, their feelings of failure, frustration, and hopelessness increase. Many skip class to avoid further embarrassment and failure, and some even drop out of school.

Since many depressed teenagers struggle socially at school, it is not uncommon to experience criticism or teasing from classmates,

A student reviews an assignment they got a low grade on. Depression can result in poor or worsening academic performance.

which can contribute to feelings of isolation.  Since their depression makes them more sensitive to criticism and failure, the rejection and humiliation can cause extreme pain. This intensifies their feelings of worthlessness, hopelessness, and anger. This pain sometimes leads to violent acts.

## SCHOOL BEHAVIOR THAT SIGNALS DEPRESSION

Many of the symptoms of depression, such as difficulty eating and sleeping or frequent crying, are more recognizable at home than at school. Teachers and other school staff may not always know which students suffer from depression, but there are some signs they can look out for, such as:

- Complaining of being bored in a class that the student used to enjoy
- Lacking energy or falling asleep in class
- Frequently requesting to see the school nurse for headaches, stomachaches, or other pains
- Expressing feelings of not being able to do anything right or feeling stupid
- Misbehaving in class and expecting to be punished
- Arguing with the teacher and fighting with classmates
- Experiencing peer problems, such as withdrawing from or becoming easily irritated by friends, or being shunned or teased by classmates
- Being unable to cope with frustration, such as angrily exploding after making mistakes
- Forgetting what has been learned or failing to finish assignments
- Talking or writing about death

## WHAT CAREGIVERS AND TEACHERS CAN DO TO HELP

In addition to treatment with psychotherapy or a combination of psychotherapy and medication, parents or caregivers and teachers can take measures to improve the well-being of depressed teenagers. When parents or legal caregivers are not present in the home or are not able to nurture their child, other significant adults in the teenager's life can support them. A grandparent, an aunt, an uncle, a family friend, a neighbor, a fellow church or synagogue member, a sports coach, or a friend's parent can often fill in for a caregiver who is unable to help. These adults can do the following:

- Make time for discussing the day's events, sharing feelings, and taking part in an activity, such as taking a walk, riding bicycles, or preparing a meal.
- Listen attentively without interrupting.
- Give clear, simple instructions, such as when asking for chores to be done, so that there are no misunderstandings.
- Give frequent praise and reward effort and achievement.
- Encourage and guide the formation of friendships by planning an outing and inviting another teenager to go along.
- Nurture a talent or a strength, such as by looking for a sports activity offered by the YMCA or a drawing class offered at an art studio.
- Encourage trying a new activity at home that can be done without an adult's help, such as cooking dinner or planting and maintaining a vegetable garden.
- Give a loving hug.

Depression can make it harder to care about or participate in hobbies or activities, but talking to an activity leader such as a sports coach could help someone find support for their depression and reengage with the activity.

Teachers can also help by doing the following:

- Create a classroom environment that fosters cooperation among students, with no tolerance for aggressive behavior or put-downs.
- Plan classroom activities that allow all students to participate equally.
- Avoid classroom activities that encourage competition.
- Frequently praise students' efforts, while keeping criticism to a minimum.

# CHAPTER SIX

# THE POWER OF SELF-ESTEEM

Self-esteem relates to the way people feel about themselves. People with high self-esteem feel good about themselves. They take pride in their abilities and accomplishments, feel self-confident, think and make decisions independently, and take on responsibilities and challenges. Other people usually receive them well.

People who have low self-esteem do not feel good about themselves. They play down their abilities and accomplishments, lack self-confidence, feel powerless, become easily frustrated, and have difficulty thinking and making decisions on their own. People tend not to receive them as well as they do others with high self-esteem.

The way people feel about themselves often goes hand in hand with the control they have over their lives. When people believe in

Feeling self-confident can sometimes make it easier to complete daunting tasks, such as presenting an assignment in front of the class.

and value themselves, they are better able to interact successfully with other people and to cope with life's disappointments. The reverse is also true. Each time someone experiences success in their relationships or in managing the ups and downs of their lives, they feel stronger and more self-confident. Their mood is brighter, and their outlook on life becomes more positive.

## Depression and Self-Esteem

Depression often affects people's perception of themselves. It shrouds them in self-doubt, guilt, and despair. They begin to see only their weaknesses and failures, which become huge and looming. Other people might then avoid the depressed person and become critical of their negative and sometimes aggressive behavior. As the people around them pull away, depressed individuals become more and more convinced that they are worthless and bad. While depressed, it is nearly impossible for them to feel important, in control, or hopeful. Their self-esteem falls to rock bottom.

## Self-Help Strategies to Boost Self-Esteem and Mood

The treatments discussed in this book help lessen the negative feelings associated with depression. As these negative feelings subside, people may find themselves with improved mood and increased energy, allowing them to take measures to begin feeling better about themselves and establishing an ongoing sense of well-being. Doing some of the things in the following list may help distract someone from negative thoughts and help them increase their self-confidence, improve their mood, and develop a brighter outlook on life. Incorporating these strategies into everyday living may also help ward off the onset of future depressive episodes. None of the actions on this list, however, should be considered a substitute for appropriate psychiatric care, psychotherapy, or medication. Not everyone will be able to take all or any of these actions either, and it's important to remember that their depression is still treatable and not their fault. When they are accessible, these options are simply a good place to start as well as helpful additions to help support one's mental health.

**Eat nutritious food and food you enjoy.** A balanced diet can provide the body with energy and foster general well-being. Food contains the nutrients necessary for good physical and mental health. The blood carries these nutrients to all the organs of the body, including the brain. It is best not to skip meals or only eat food with poor nutritional value.

**Exercise.** Exercise can help ease restlessness and increase brain chemicals called endorphins, which elevate mood. Exercise also raises the heart rate and increases the amount of oxygen in the body, which contributes to good physical health. Being strong or able to do the physical things somebody wants to do can also increase their self-esteem.

**Get adequate rest.** Ideally, a full night's sleep is best. But when sleep is interrupted or insufficient, resting or napping during the day can help.

**Talk with family members or other loved ones.** Setting aside regular time to talk with family members, friends, or other loved ones about the day or your feelings can help strengthen relationships and keep people aware of your emotional state. Solid relationships are important in preventing future episodes of depression.

**Reduce stress.** Research has shown that our attitude toward life can alter the amount of chemicals in the brain that affect the overall health of our bodies. If we feel anxious, for example, our bodies produce extra stress hormones, which can make us sick. The saying "Laughter is the best medicine" rings true. Laughing keeps the level of stress hormones down and can help when coping with difficult life events. Watching comedy shows on television or renting funny movies can lighten your mood. Listening to soothing music can also help reduce stress. Additionally, learning to set appropriate boundaries and say "no" when you are already stressed or overworked can go a long way towards reducing your stress.

**Avoid procrastination.** Procrastination breeds stress. Worrying about unfinished assignments or chores can burden the mind and

People laugh while watching something. Both laughter and spending time with people who support them can help someone feel less stressed or overwhelmed with negative feelings.

create tension. Tackling tasks promptly can help to avoid excess anxiety. If you notice that you are procrastinating a lot or more than usual, remember that procrastination can also be a sign of depression.

**Allow room for imperfections**. Everyone makes mistakes, and everyone has shortcomings. Trying to be perfect creates a lot of unnecessary worry. Accepting failure and being willing to try again can be much healthier. Setting accessible goals can help. When a goal is attainable, you're more likely to achieve it, and that success bolsters self-esteem.

**Keep a journal.** Worrying can interfere with concentration and completion of tasks, including school assignments. Making a list of your worries and writing down the feelings that accompany them can often help to relieve the mind, make problems seem more manageable, and even help you come up with solutions to some problems.

**Replace negative thoughts with positive thoughts.** Replacing negative thoughts with positive thoughts, such as good memories and future plans, can help break a pattern of negative thinking. Listing these positive thoughts on a piece of paper and then reading them when negative thoughts cloud the mind can improve a low mood.

**Make a list of strengths.** A list of strengths can serve the same purpose. Strengths may include talents such as being good in sports or playing a musical instrument well; achievements such as winning a race or learning how to bake a moist chocolate cake; special personality qualities such as being especially patient with

A young person writes in a journal. Journaling can not only help settle some current and future worries, but it also lets people record important memories and look back on their days or feelings.

young children or older adults; or unique and exciting interests such as knowing a lot about astronomy or animals. Focusing on strengths can help lift falling self-esteem.

**Spend time with a pet.** Playing with a pet can also elevate your mood. The exercise you may get from it and time spent outside can help clear your mind. Playing with a pet, even someone else's, can help relieve stress and can often shift the focus away from life's problems. The act of petting itself can be quite soothing for the person and the animal. This is part of why many universities and hospitals now offer pet therapy for stress relief.

**Plan outings.** Going out with family or friends and planning activities in advance can provide a welcome break from the daily worries of work and school. Outings to a concert, movie, museum, beach, lake, or amusement park can be uplifting. Even taking a walk with a friend can help relieve stress and give you an activity to look forward to.

**Get involved in an enjoyable activity.** Taking a class or participating in an activity or hobby you enjoy, such as dancing, gardening, cooking, sewing, sailing, skiing, or drawing, can bring joy. Many activities can also be done with other people, which can help you establish and maintain friendships.

**Join a club.** Many schools offer after-school clubs, such as drama, photography, gardening, or chess. You might develop new interests and talents and form new friendships through participating in these clubs.

**Get a job.** The benefits of taking on a part-time job can include earning spending money, mastering a new skill, and working with other people. Not only can holding a job potentially keep the mind positively focused, but some jobs can also provide a sense of accomplishment. However, taking on a job when someone is already

A young adult plays piano with an older adult. Volunteering at places where someone works directly with other people can also be a good way to build and connect with community.

really busy might result in them being more stressed out overall. It's important to evaluate your personal situation and how much additional stress you can handle before applying for jobs.

**Organize belongings.** Sometimes straightening a bedroom and organizing belongings can bring about a sense of well-being. Drawers and closets can be tidied, for example. Videos, music albums, and books can be organized on a shelf. Putting together an album of your favorite photographs can also bring joy.

**Do something nice for someone.** Doing a household chore without being asked or baking cookies for a family member or friend can help create positive feelings both in yourself and others. Even

giving someone a compliment can feel good. The added benefit
of opening up to others is that they are likely to open up to you
in return.

**Do volunteer work.** Spending a few hours each week or each
month doing volunteer work can be extremely gratifying. Nursing
homes, hospitals, libraries, and charitable organizations all
welcome help from young people. In addition to feeling good about
helping others, you may learn a skill that can be used in a paying
job someday.

All these suggestions are helpful, but they can also be
overwhelming to look at all at once. If you or someone you know is
struggling to know where to start, a mental health professional can
also help figure out which steps are most appropriate and how to
implement them.

# THE FUTURE OF DEPRESSION

Researchers continue to study how depression works and to test new treatments. For example, in the early 2020s, researchers were conducting studies to see if controlled doses of ketamine, an anesthetic, could effectively combat treatment-resistant depression. The results were promising, and experts continue to study the long-term effects of ketamine treatment. As research continues into how to best treat depression, there is hope that more and more people will be able to manage their disorder.

Depression affects many people in the world every single day. It is a serious mental illness that can severely impact somebody's quality of life and ability to interact with their friends, family, community, and the rest of the outside world. Depression can be debilitating, but with the proper treatment and support, it can be managed and treated. Having depression may feel lonely and

# CELEBRITIES AND DEPRESSION

Depression can affect anybody, no matter where they've come from or what kind of life they lead. Depression is a serious illness, but it doesn't have to put your life on hold. In recent years, more and more celebrities have begun to speak out about their struggles with mental health on social media. Some of these celebrities are:

- Dwayne "The Rock" Johnson
- Lady Gaga
- Selena Gomez
- Jim Carrey
- Kerry Washington
- Dolly Parton
- Demi Lovato
- Elliot Page
- Billie Eilish
- Lili Reinhart
- Sophie Turner
- Justin Bieber

By speaking out about their own struggles and experiences with mental health, many of these celebrities hope to share a more human side of depression and show how people with depression can continue to live full and meaningful lives.

isolating at times, but people with this or any other mental illness are never truly alone. There are always resources and help for those who are struggling.

**anorexia nervosa:** an eating disorder characterized by an intense fear of being overweight that causes the individual to eat very little food and experience dangerous weight loss

**attention deficit hyperactivity disorder:** a condition that involves several related symptoms that fall into three main categories: inattention, impulsiveness, and hyperactivity

**atypical depression:** a form of depression characterized by oversleeping and overeating, decreased energy, and extreme sensitivity to rejection

**axon:** a thin projection on the end of a neuron that transmits messages to other neurons

**behavioral therapy:** a type of psychotherapy that treats depression as learned behavior that can be unlearned

**bipolar disorder:** alternating periods of feeling extremely happy and extremely depressed

**bulimia nervosa:** an eating disorder characterized by bingeing on food and then purging by vomiting, using laxatives or diuretics, or exercising excessively

**cognitive therapy:** a type of psychotherapy based on the idea that people who think negatively about themselves, the world, and the future will develop feelings of despair. Patients are taught to replace negative thoughts with positive thoughts.

**dopamine:** a neurotransmitter that helps to regulate mood

**dysthymia:** a mild form of depression that lasts two or more years

**electroconvulsive therapy:** a treatment for severe depression that involves passing a low-voltage electrical current through the brain; also called shock therapy

**family therapy:** a type of psychotherapy that involves the entire family participating in a therapy session to discuss problems and improve communication

**interpersonal therapy:** a type of psychotherapy that is based on the idea that people become depressed because of problems that arise within relationships with family or friends

**monoamine oxidase:** an enzyme in the nervous system that breaks down neurotransmitters

**neurons:** nerve cells

**neurotransmitters:** brain chemicals that carry messages from one neuron to another

**norepinephrine:** a type of neurotransmitter that helps to regulate mood

**obsessive-compulsive disorder:** an anxiety disorder characterized by a persistent thought or impulse (obsession) to perform some activity repetitively (compulsion)

**psychiatrist:** a medical doctor who specializes in the treatment of mental, emotional, and behavioral disorders

**psychologist:** a person educated in the science of the mind and behavior who is trained in counseling people with mental, emotional, and/or behavioral disorders

**psychotherapy:** the treatment of emotional disorders that involves talking with a therapist to understand and resolve conflicts

**receptors:** molecules on the surface of neurons that receive messages from neurotransmitters

**remission:** the reduction or disappearance of the signs and symptoms of a disorder, illness, or disease

**reuptake:** reabsorption of a neurotransmitter by the neuron that released it

**seasonal affective disorder:** a form of depression that usually occurs during the fall and winter months when there is decreased sunlight

**self-esteem:** confidence in and satisfaction with one's self

**serotonin:** a type of neurotransmitter that helps to regulate mood

**statistically significant:** when the results found in a set of data are not explainable by chance alone

**suicide:** the act or instance of taking one's own life voluntarily or intentionally

**synapse:** a tiny, fluid-filled gap between neurons across which messages are carried by neurotransmitters

**therapist:** a professional who works with people to solve problems, discuss feelings, or change behavior. Psychiatrists, psychologists, and social workers are therapists.

# SOURCE NOTES

19–20  "The serotonin theory . . . to do with?": Adam Miller, "Have We Been
Treating Depression the Wrong Way for Decades?," *CBC News*,
updated August 13, 2022, https://www.cbc.ca/news/health
/depression-antidepressants-review-serotonin-1.6548219.

47  "Don't be afraid . . . quality of life.": "Depression versus Sadness:
When to Talk with Your Doctor," Doctors of Osteopathic Medicine,
accessed October 30, 2023, https://findado.osteopathic.org
/depression-versus-sadness-when-to-talk-with-your-doctor.

56  "In people who . . . helps relieve depression.": "Exercise Is an All-
Natural Treatment to Fight Depression," Harvard Health Publishing,
February 2, 2021, https://www.health.harvard.edu/mind-and
-mood/exercise-is-an-all-natural-treatment-to-fight-depression.

# SELECTED BIBLIOGRAPHY

"Adolescent Health." Centers for Disease Control and Prevention. Updated July 25, 2023. https://www.cdc.gov/nchs/fastats/adolescent-health.htm.

Brent, David. "Treatment-Resistant Depression in Adolescents." *UPMC Synergies*. Presented December 10, 2018. https://www.upmcphysicianresources.com /-/media/physicianresources/pdf-publications/psychiatry/synergies_winter _2018_07_final.pdf.

Cohen, Sandy. "Suicide Rate Highest among Teens and Young Adults." UCLA Health, March 15, 2022. https://www.uclahealth.org/news/suicide-rate -highest-among-teens-and-young-adults.

"Definition of Treatment-Resistant Depression in the Medicare Population." Centers for Medicare and Medicaid Services. Accessed June 11, 2023. https:// www.cms.gov/medicare-coverage-database/view/technology-assessments .aspx?TAId=105&bc=AAAQAAAAAAAA.

"Depression." Medscape. Updated January 5, 2023. https://emedicine .medscape.com/article/286759-overview.

Levinson, Douglas F., and Walter E. Nichols. "Major Depression and Genetics." Stanford Medicine. Accessed June 11, 2023. https://med.stanford.edu /depressiongenetics/mddandgenes.html.

"Major Depression." National Institute of Mental Health. Updated July 2023. https://www.nimh.nih.gov/health/statistics/major-depression.

Moriarty, Andrew S., et al. "Predicting and Preventing Relapse of Depression in Primary Care." *British Journal of General Practice* 70, no. 691 (2020): 54–55. https://doi.org/10.3399/bjgp20X707753.

"SAMHSA Announces National Survey on Drug Use and Health (NSDUH) Results Detailing Mental Illness and Substance Use Levels in 2021." US Department of Health and Human Resources, January 4, 2023. https://www.hhs.gov/about /news/2023/01/04/samhsa-announces-national-survey-drug-use-health -results-detailing-mental-illness-substance-use-levels-2021.html.

"Some Facts about Suicide and Depression." Washington, DC: American Association for Suicidology, 2009.

Torchinsky, Rina. "Nearly Half of LGBTQ Youth Seriously Considered Suicide, Survey Finds." MPR News, May 5, 2022. https://www.npr.org/2022/05/05/1096920693/lgbtq-youth-thoughts-of-suicide-trevor-project-survey.

"2022 National Survey on LGBTQ Youth Mental Health." Trevor Project. Accessed June 11, 2023. https://www.thetrevorproject.org/survey-2022.

Villaroel, Maria A., and Emily P. Terlizzi. "Symptoms of Depression among Adults: United States, 2019." National Center for Health Statistics Data Brief, no. 379. Hyattsville, MD: National Center for Health Statistics, 2020.

"What Causes Depression?" Harvard Health Publishing, January 10, 2022. https://www.health.harvard.edu/mind-and-mood/what-causes-depression.

Wilson, Sylia, and Nathalie M. Dumornay. "Rising Rates of Adolescent Depression in the United States: Challenges and Opportunities in the 2020s." *Journal of Adolescent Health* 70, no. 3 (2022): 354–355. https://doi.org/10.1016%2Fj.jadohealth.2021.12.003.

American Academy of Child and Adolescent Psychiatry
http://www.aacap.org
The American Academy of Child and Adolescent Psychiatry is dedicated to educating families, teachers, and other concerned individuals about mental health issues facing young people, promoting early identification and treatment, and encouraging funding for scientifically based research.

Depression and Bipolar Support Alliance
http://www.dbsalliance.org
The alliance educates the public about depression and bipolar disorder and strives to help patients and their families find help. In addition to state organizations and local chapters, it offers extensive online resources and 450 support groups nationwide.

The International Foundation for Research and Education on Depression
http://www.ifred.org
This foundation helps to further research into the causes of depression. It also supports those dealing with depression and works to educate the public and combat the stigma associated with depression. Its website features many resources including a list of international resources and suicide hotlines.

Mental Health America (MHA)
https://mhanational.org
MHA has more than three hundred affiliates nationwide. The organization strives to educate the public about mental health issues, promote research in this field, and provide community service for people with mental illnesses and their families.

National Alliance on Mental Illness (NAMI)
https://nami.org
NAMI is the largest grassroots organization in the United States dedicated to improving the lives of individuals and families affected by mental illness. They focus on support, education, and advocacy. In addition to the national organization, there are more than six hundred state and local groups across the US. Trained volunteers monitor NAMI's information helpline, (800) 950-6264, to provide information, referrals, and support to anyone who has questions about or is affected by serious mental illness.

National Suicide Prevention Lifeline
(800) 273-TALK (8255) or 988
https://988lifeline.org
If you or someone you know is in a suicidal crisis or emotional distress, the trained counselors at this organization can help. Calling the number connects you to the lifeline network closest to your location. The service is free and confidential and is available twenty-four hours a day, seven days a week.

## Books for Young Adults


Buckey, A. W. *Teens and Depression*. San Diego: ReferencePoint Press, 2021.

Hyman, Bruce M., Cherry Pedrick, and Tabitha Moriarty. *More Than Stress: Understanding Anxiety Disorders*. Minneapolis: Twenty-First Century Books, 2023.

*Life inside my Mind: 31 Authors Share Their Personal Struggles*. New York: Simon Pulse, 2018.

Mental Health America. *Where to Start: A Survival Guide to Anxiety, Depression, and Other Mental Health Challenges*. New York: Rocky Pond Books, 2023.

Scientific American Editors. *Navigating Anxiety and Depression: Scientific American Explores Big Ideas*. New York: Rosen, 2023.

Sonenklar, Carol, and Tabitha Moriarty. *Not Just about Food; Understanding Eating Disorders*. Minneapolis: Twenty-First Century Books, 2023.


## Books for Parents and Family Members


Duffy, John. *Parenting the New Teen in the Age of Anxiety: A Complete Guide to Your Child's Stressed, Depressed, Expanded, Amazing Adolescence*. Coral Gables, FL: Mango Publishing, 2019.

Lewis, Lisa L. *The Sleep-Deprived Teen: Why Our Teenagers Are so Tired, and How Parents and Schools Can Help Them Thrive*. Coral Gables, FL: Mango Publishing, 2022.

Noonan, Susan J. *Helping Others with Depression: Words to Say, Things to Do*. Baltimore: Johns Hopkins University Press, 2021.

## Websites

Brain and Behavior Research Foundation

https://www.bbrfoundation.org

This foundation raises money from donors around the world and invests it directly in research projects in mental health. Its website provides information on depression, anxiety, obsessive-compulsive disorder, eating disorders, and other disorders, including the latest research, articles, and information for people with these disorders and those who want to help them.

Mental Health: American Psychological Association (APA)

https://www.apa.org/topics/mental-health

The APA is a scientific and professional organization that represents psychology in the United States. It is the largest association of psychologists worldwide. The organization works to share its members' psychological knowledge to benefit society and improve people's lives. Its mental health web page offers resources, information, and more on various mental health topics.

Mental Health: The Trevor Project

https://www.thetrevorproject.org/resources/category/mental-health

The Trevor Project seeks to end suicide among LGBTQ+ youth. Their website offers many materials for young people, including this web page featuring articles on resources, information, and statistics about mental health among LGBTQ+ people.

Teen Depression: Mayo Clinic

http://www.mayoclinic.com/health/teen-depression/DS01188

The Mayo Clinic, one of the best-known nonprofit medical institutions in the United States, has comprehensive information on depression, including information on symptoms, causes, risk factors, complications, tests and diagnosis, treatment, lifestyle remedies, alternative medicine, coping and support, and prevention.

TeensHealth

https://kidshealth.org/en/teens

TeensHealth is part of the Nemours Foundation, one of the largest nonprofit organizations devoted to adolescent health. The site provides information on a wide range of physical, emotional, and behavioral conditions that affect young people.

# INDEX


antidepressants
monoamine oxidase inhibitors (MAOIs), 58, 60
selective serotonin reuptake inhibitors (SSRIs), 58–59, 61
tricyclic antidepressants, 58
anxiety, 14, 34
anxiety (symptom), 19, 37, 40, 62, 92–93
attention deficit hyperactivity disorder, 38–39
atypical depression, 24

bipolar disorder, 23–24, 60
brain chemistry, 20–21, 26

causes, 16–27
biological, 19–21
environmental, 21–22
genetic, 18–19, 46
conduct disorder, 37–38

diagnosis, 30, 42–47
coping with, 46–47
interviews, 45–46
patient history, 44–45
physical examination, 44
psychological tests, 45
diet, 24–25, 31, 48, 91–92
dysthymia, 22–23

eating disorders, 39–40
electroconvulsive shock therapy, 49, 63
exercise, 48–49, 56–57, 92, 95

generalized anxiety disorder, 35

genetic factors
in depression, 18–19
in suicide, 72–73

hereditary
*See* genetic factors
hospitalization, 65

ketamine, 98

learning disabilities, 39, 75–76
LGBTQ+ people, 9, 12–13, 71–72, 75
light therapy, 25–26
lithium, 60

medication
*See* antidepressants
mental health professionals, 43–46, 50, 54, 65, 77, 97

neurons, 16–17, 19–20, 58
neurotransmitters
dopamine, 19–20, 61
norepinephrine, 19–20, 58, 61
serotonin, 19–20, 58–59, 61

obsessive-compulsive disorder, 35–36, 58
oppositional defiant disorder, 37–38

phobias, 36
postpartum depression, 26–27
post-traumatic stress disorder, 36–37
psychological tests, 45
psychosis, 26–27, 30, 41, 65

psychotherapy, 47–56, 66, 87
  choosing a therapist, 53–54
  cognitive behavioral therapy, 51
  family therapy, 52
  group therapy, 52–53
  interpersonal therapy, 51–52

rates of depression, 7–13
resources, 54, 65, 75

sadness, 13, 22–23, 28–29, 84
school performance, 21, 31, 34,
    45–46, 74–76, 83–86
seasonal affective disorder, 25–26
self-confidence and self-esteem, 29,
    47–48, 89–97
self-destructive behavior, 12–13, 29,
    47, 65
separation anxiety disorder, 35
sexual violence, 12–13, 36, 73, 81
substance use disorder, 40–41, 65,
    74

suicide
  effect on family and friends,
    76–77
  help for, 65, 77–79
  LGBTQ+ people and factors, 9, 12,
    71–72, 75
  warning signs, 69–70
support system, 50–51, 75, 77–80,
    87, 92
symptoms, 14–15, 19, 29–34, 44,
    83–86

transcranial magnetic stimulation, 49
treatment
  *See* hospitalization, medication,
    psychotherapy, transcranial
    magnetic stimulation

## ABOUT THE AUTHORS

Wendy Moragne is a former teacher and writer who now practices as an attorney.

Tabitha Moriarty is a medical student living in Atlanta, Georgia.

## PHOTO ACKNOWLEDGMENTS

Image credits: dmbaker/Getty Images, p. 5; Michael Ciaglo/Getty Images, p. 11; RealPeopleGroup/Getty Images, p. 15; VectorMine/Shutterstock, p. 17; Pikovit/Shutterstock, p. 20; Image Point Fr/Shutterstock, p. 25; Daisy Daisy/Shutterstock, p. 32; Wavebreak Media Ltd/Alamy, p. 34; Cyndi Monaghan/Getty Images, p. 36; Kathy deWitt/Alamy, p. 38; AleksandrYu/Getty Images, p. 41; Jim Holden/Alamy, p. 43; Phynart Studio/Getty Images, p. 50; SeventyFour/Shutterstock, p. 53; Jacek Chabraszewski/Shutterstock, p. 57; Morsa Images/Getty Images, p. 62; Tirachard Kumtanom/Shutterstock, p. 66; Maskot/Getty Images, p. 68; FG Trade/Getty Images, p. 71; DCPhoto/Alamy, p. 79; globalmoments/Getty Images, p. 82; Pheelings media/Shutterstock, p. 85; digitalskillet/Shutterstock, p. 88; SDI Productions/Getty Images, p. 90; Burak Fatsa/Getty Images, p. 93; Odua Images/Shutterstock, p. 94; PamelaJoeMcFarlane/Getty Images, p. 96.

Cover: nimito/Shutterstock; Besfamilnaya/Shutterstock.